RAND
CORPORATION

# The Changing Role of Criminal Law in Controlling Corporate Behavior

James M. Anderson, Ivan Waggoner

For more information on this publication, visit www.rand.org/t/rr412

Library of Congress Cataloging-in-Publication Data

Anderson, James M., author.
The changing role of criminal law in controlling corporate behavior / James M. Anderson, Ivan Waggoner.
pages cm
Includes bibliographical references.
ISBN 978-0-8330-8786-7 (pbk. : alk. paper)
1. Criminal liability of juristic persons—United States. 2. Tort liability of corporations—United States. 3. Corporate governance—Law and legislation—United States—Criminal provisions. I. Waggoner, Ivan, author. II. Title.

KF9236.5.A93 2014
345.73'04—dc23

2014047644

Published by the RAND Corporation, Santa Monica, Calif.


*Cover image via fl1photo/Fotolia.*



The RAND Corporation is a research organization that develops solutions to public policy challenges to help make communities throughout the world safer and more secure, healthier and more prosperous. RAND is nonprofit, nonpartisan, and committed to the public interest.

RAND's publications do not necessarily reflect the opinions of its research clients and sponsors.

## Support RAND

Make a tax-deductible charitable contribution at
www.rand.org/giving/contribute

www.rand.org

# Preface

This report examines the use of criminal law in the corporate context. The research had three primary goals: (1) trace the development of the application of criminal law to corporate activities, (2) identify and analyze empirical trends with respect to the use of criminal law in this context, and (3) use this research to develop guidance for policymakers in this area.

This report should be of interest to policymakers and researchers who are interested in the advantages and disadvantages of using criminal law to control organizational and corporate behavior.

The report builds on a body of research by the RAND Institute for Civil Justice and the RAND Center for Corporate Ethics and Governance. From the effects of the Foreign Corrupt Practices Act[1] to the effect of the Federal Sentencing Guidelines on corporate governance, the center has been publishing independent analyses to aid policymakers in achieving an empirically grounded understanding of the relevant issues.

## RAND Institute for Civil Justice

The RAND Institute for Civil Justice (ICJ) is dedicated to improving the civil justice system by supplying policymakers and the public with rigorous and nonpartisan research. Its studies identify trends in litigation and inform policy choices concerning liability, compensation,

[1] Public Law 95-213, Foreign Corrupt Practices Act, December 19, 1977.

regulation, risk management, and insurance. The institute builds on a long tradition of RAND Corporation research characterized by an interdisciplinary, empirical approach to public policy issues and rigorous standards of quality, objectivity, and independence.

ICJ research is supported by pooled grants from a range of sources, including corporations, trade and professional associations, individuals, government agencies, and private foundations. All its reports are subject to peer review and disseminated widely to policymakers, practitioners in law and business, other researchers, and the public.

The ICJ is part of RAND Justice, Infrastructure, and Environment, a division of the RAND Corporation dedicated to improving policy and decisionmaking in a wide range of policy domains, including civil and criminal justice, infrastructure protection and homeland security, transportation and energy policy, and environmental and natural resources policy.

Questions or comments about this report should be sent to the project leader, James M. Anderson (James_Anderson@rand.org). For more information on the Institute for Civil Justice, see http://www.rand.org/icj or contact the director (icjdirector@rand.org).

# Contents

# Figures and Table

## Figures

## Table

# Summary

Corporations are immensely powerful entities, capable of both greatly increasing human welfare and greatly harming it. It is therefore important that both corporations and the people who work on their behalf are appropriately regulated and controlled. What should the role of criminal liability be in controlling corporate behavior, and how can the execution of that role be improved?

On the one hand, corporations have enormous power, and, when a corporation causes harm, there is a natural instinct to apply criminal sanctions, society's most serious expression of moral disapproval. In the wake of a harm in which a corporation had a prominent role (e.g., the savings and loan crisis of the early 1990s, the revelation of Enron accounting, and the Great Recession), there are often calls for an increased use of the criminal law to tame corporate excesses. On the other hand, criminal liability has historically usually required criminal intent, a concept that applies oddly to a legal construction, such as a corporation. And more recently, critics have decried what they have termed the overcriminalization of corporate behavior, suggesting that there has been an overreliance on the use of criminal law in this context.

This report addresses the use of criminal sanctions to control corporate behavior. This includes both prosecutions of the corporation itself and criminal prosecutions of employees for actions taken on behalf of corporations. We do not address criminal sanctions imposed on individuals for actions directly taken to benefit themselves, e.g., embezzlement.

To address the question of the proper role of criminal sanctions, we (1) describe the current state of the use of criminal sanctions in controlling corporate behavior, (2) describe how the current regime developed, and (3) offer suggestions about how the use of criminal sanctions to control corporate behavior might be improved.

Our approach was two-fold: We first reviewed the literature and synthesized what we know—and what we do not yet know—about the role of criminal law in controlling the behavior of corporations and the people who work in them. We then drew on empirical data to examine trends in criminal prosecutions. We organized our results in terms of these specific questions:

- How did criminal liability, which historically focused on individual wrongdoing, come to be applied to a legal construction, the corporation? What lessons can we draw from that history?
- What are the recent developments in this area?
- What are the quantitative trends in criminal prosecutions of corporate activity over the past 25 years?
- What policy reforms should be considered to address any shortcomings in the application of corporate criminal liability?

## Emergence of Corporate Criminal Liability

Originally, corporations were immune from criminal sanctions and criminal liability. In the second half of the 19th century, however, criminal law began to expand to corporations. Although critics frequently decried the odd fit between the intentionality usually required in criminal law and how it might be applied to a corporate entity, prosecutors, legislators, and judges upheld such prosecutions largely on pragmatic grounds. Few argued that corporations *deserved* punishment—that is, few called upon moral arguments to justify punishment that have traditionally supported criminal sanctions. Instead, defenders of corporate criminal liability used pragmatic arguments: Criminal sanctions were held to be necessary because of the opacity of corporations to outside scrutiny and the inability of outside parties to identify the most culpable parties. The threat of criminal sanctions, it was argued, could also help prevent corporate wrongdoing: Such sanctions made it more likely that corporations would comply with regulations. By the early 20th century, corporate criminal liability was well established, with the courts recognizing that corporations could be found guilty even of crimes that ordinarily required a specific criminal intent.

## Reforming Corporations from Within

The Sentencing Reform Act of 1984 and the Federal Sentencing Guidelines for Organizations of 1991 reinforced a shift toward using sanctions to motivate corporations to develop compliance programs.[2] At first, the emphasis was on developing these programs and bringing in outside corporate monitors as a condition of probation, after the corporation was convicted. Over time, however, compliance programs and acquiescence to restructuring moved up in the criminal process to become criteria on which a decision to prosecute was made. The downfall of Arthur Andersen, which highlighted the potentially firm-ending risks of taking a case to trial and the enormous collateral damage that can occur with aggressive prosecution, led to the greatly expanded use of nonprosecution and deferred prosecution agreements—agreements to forgo or delay prosecution in return for structural reforms. Over time, these voluntary agreements became standard substitutes for the traditional criminal process of conviction and punishment.

Although these agreements have allowed prosecutors to accomplish their objectives of reforming the corporation without the expense, delay, and risk of trial, they have also created their own complications, including the lack of judicial scrutiny, the lack of institutional competence of outside monitors, and the problems that are raised by partly outsourcing of the prosecutorial function to the corporations themselves. In effect, they result in the partial privatization of a historically public function—investigating and prosecuting potential violations of the criminal law.

---

[2] Public Law 98-473, joint resolution for continuing appropriations, October 12, 1984.

## Trends in Prosecutions

Comparing several sources of data to better understand recent trends, we found that convictions of corporate actors have been declining since the 1990s (see Figure S.1).[3] This decline continued through the 2008 financial crisis and appears to have stabilized for now, at a rate much lower than enforcement during the 1990s. This evidence confirms our observation that criminal law in the corporate context has evolved from

**Figure S.1**
**Corporations Convicted in Federal Courts, 1994–2010**

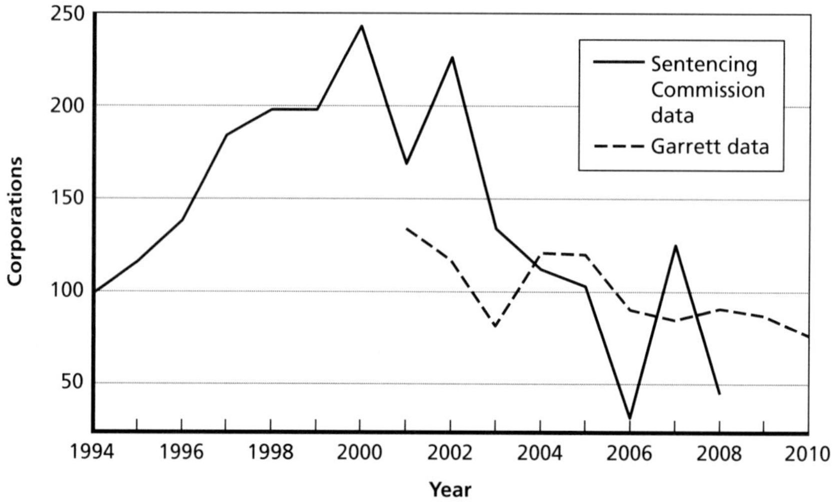


SOURCES: U.S. Sentencing Commission, 1999; Garrett and Ashley, undated.
RAND *RR412-S.1*

---

[3] The data sources include *Federal Court Cases: Integrated Data Base* (Federal Judicial Center, *Federal Court Cases: Integrated Data Base*, Ann Arbor, Mich.: Inter-university Consortium for Political and Social Research, 2011); U.S. Sentencing Commission data on corporations sentenced in federal courts (U.S. Sentencing Commission, *Organizations Convicted in Federal Criminal Courts, 1999–2008*, Washington, D.C., 1999); *TRACFED*, compiled by the Transactional Records Access Clearinghouse (TRAC), a research center at Syracuse University (TRAC, "TRACFED," undated [a]); and a database compiled by Brandon L. Garrett and Jon Ashley of the University of Virginia, based on media searches of corporate convictions and prosecutions (Brandon L. Garrett and Jon Ashley, "Federal Organizational Plea Agreements," Charlottesville, Va.: University of Virginia School of Law, undated).

prosecuting offenders to encouraging corporations themselves to police misconduct. The decrease in the number of firms convicted coincides with a striking increase in the number of deferred-prosecution agreements (DPAs) and nonprosecution agreements (NPAs) that prosecutors reached with firms suspected of criminal behavior, as shown in Figure S.2.

There are two exceptions to the overall decline in convictions: litigation based on the Sarbanes-Oxley Act of 2002[4] and the Foreign Corrupt Practices Act. In the data for post-2004, we found a substantial increase in the prosecution of individual defendants convicted under at least one of the criminal provisions under the Sarbanes-Oxley Act. Over that same period, Foreign Corrupt Practices Act prosecutions of corporations by both the U.S. Securities and Exchange Commission (SEC) and the U.S. Department of Justice (DOJ) also steadily

**Figure S.2**
**Deferred and Nonprosecution Agreements, 1992–2010**

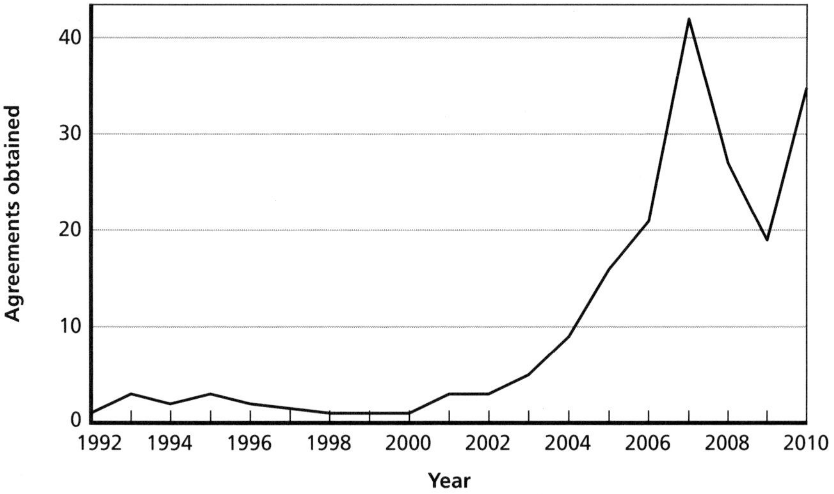


SOURCE: Brandon L. Garrett and Jon Ashley, "Federal Organizational Prosecution Agreements," last updated October 27, 2014.
RAND *RR412-S.2*

---

4 Public Law 107-204, Sarbanes-Oxley Act of 2002, July 30, 2002.

increased: we found a total of 265 investigations and charges, with nine times as many enforcement actions initiated in 2011 than in 2004. This increase reflects the renewed emphasis at DOJ on curbing global corruption. Debarment and suspension proceedings, which prevent or impair an indicted or convicted firm from doing business with some part of the federal government, have also increased dramatically. These trends may help explain any perceptions of increased criminal prosecutorial activity.

What do these trends tell us about the changing role of criminal law in regulating and controlling corporate activity? The evidence is mixed. On the one hand, with the exceptions of the application of Sarbanes-Oxley and the Foreign Corrupt Practices Act, the number of criminal prosecutions of corporations has declined in recent years, suggesting less formal prosecutorial activity rather than more. On the other hand, the use of DPAs, NPAs, and debarment activity has increased sharply, suggesting that the threat of criminal action is still playing an important role in controlling behavior in this context.

The trends described in this report have led to an odd juncture in the evolution of this area of the law. Corporations and their directors are hesitant to directly challenge prosecutorial theories for fear of the collateral consequences. Federal agencies are increasing debarment and suspension proceedings in an effort to minimize waste and fraud. The result is the huge increase in DPAs and NPAs, which lack some of the key benefits of public law. Typically, these agreements involve little or no judicial oversight of prosecutorial activity, no formal fact-finding, and often the hiring of private-sector compliance monitors. As a result, there may be greatly reduced development of the common law. Occasionally, NPAs and DPAs have contained questionable provisions requiring companies to take certain political positions or, in one case, endow a chair at the prosecutor's alma mater. With little judicial or prosecutorial oversight, corporations may face pressure to investigate individual wrongdoers in order to be perceived by prosecutors as cooperating and to avoid criminal liability on the part of the corporation. The result is the partial privatization of corporate criminal law.

## Lessons for Policymakers, Prosecutors, and Judges

### Recognize That Criminal Sanctions Are Instrumental Tools and Not Moral Judgments

Although the use of criminal sanctions applied to corporations and individuals without criminal intent is long established and may be justified on pragmatic grounds, this pragmatic justification has important implications. Over the 1,000-year history of Anglo-American criminal law, courts have usually required a culpable intent as a prerequisite to inflicting criminal punishment. Doing so is generally consistent with the criminal law's function as society's strongest collective expression of its disapproval. When a community drops that requirement and uses criminal law purely for instrumental means, it should be certain that these ends truly justify the means.

Although the benefits of using criminal penalties to provide incentives to comply with the law are obvious, the costs may be less so. The collateral consequences of prosecuting a corporation for criminal wrongdoing can be vast and difficult to predict. Similarly, criminally punishing individuals who are guilty of poor judgment, bad luck, or of having employees who broke the law may create beneficial incentives, but only at the cost of diluting the collective significance of the criminal sanction. Lawmakers should be reluctant to pass statutes that punish without proof of criminal intent, courts should be reluctant to interpret statutes in ways that ignore criminal intent, and prosecutors should bring such prosecutions sparingly.

### Have Judges Review Deferred and Nonprosecution Agreements

Some of the potential problems we have raised with the proliferation of DPAs and NPAs can be mitigated by judicial oversight. This will provide an independent party to review the value of the agreement and ensure that abuses do not occur. Just as a plea agreement in a standard criminal prosecution against an individual defendant has to be reviewed by an appropriate federal judge, so should these agreements be reviewed for fairness and to ensure that they are in the public interest. This practice would provide some assurance that the agreements are genuinely in the public interest and might allow third parties affected by the agreements to air their objections in a neutral forum. Policymakers should give serious consideration to requiring that every DPA and NPA be reviewed by an appropriate federal judge. This practice would provide additional transparency and reassure the public that justice was being served.

#### Carefully Review Debarment Provisions

Debarment proceedings have increased sharply in the past four years. Although they may be justified, the consequences can be so severe that they may discourage corporations from taking even very strong cases to trial and risk a conviction that would trigger debarment. Policymakers should carefully review debarment policies that automatically require a licensing agency or an entity of government to refuse to do business with or license a corporation that has been indicted or convicted. Rather than a *per se* rule that requires this potentially catastrophic outcome for the corporation on any conviction for certain offenses, the decision should be made on a case-by-case basis by the relevant governmental agency, depending on the severity of the allegations made and their relevance to the domain of the governmental entity.

#### Consider Substituting the Use of Civil Sanctions

In many cases, civil sanctions that include a formal fact-finding might function just as well as—if not better than—criminal sanctions. One rationale for using criminal law against corporations has been that it was necessary to identify illegal actions cloaked in the opacity of an organization. It is not clear why appropriately stiff civil sanctions cannot play a similar role. Even some of the expressive functions of the criminal law can be fulfilled if there is explicit fact-finding and a finding of culpability on the part of the organization. Civil sanctions could also sidestep some of the potentially catastrophic reputational and collateral harm associated with criminal sanctions and could therefore result in more-appropriate challenges by accused companies and their directors. Structural reform and compliance programs could also be motivated by enhanced civil, rather than criminal, sanctions. In this way, the national community might better harmonize its system of justice in this unique context.

# Acknowledgments

We acknowledge and thank many people who contributed to this research. Members of the RAND Institute for Civil Justice (ICJ) Board of Overseers were extremely helpful in their comments. We thank Paul Heaton and James N. Dertouzos for their leadership of ICJ during this project and Pamela Calig for her able administration of the project. We thank Jennifer H. Arlen for her helpful comments on the project and Joseph W. Doherty and Ingrid V. Eagly for their assistance, as well as the UCLA-RAND Center for Law and Public Policy. Sarah Hauer made numerous helpful edits and successfully reconciled competing versions of the document on at least three different operating systems. Lisa Bernard did a masterful job editing difficult prose. We thank Susan M. Gates for her assistance in moving this project through the quality-assurance process. We thank Samuel W. Buell of Duke University School of Law and Nicholas M. Pace of ICJ for their careful and thorough critiques of earlier drafts of this report, as well as many others with whom we have discussed this topic.

James Anderson would like to thank Katherine Brownlee for her support and comments on the project.

Ivan Waggoner would like to thank Mark Motivans of the Bureau of Justice Statistics for his assistance with the data used throughout this report.

# Abbreviations

| | |
|---|---|
| BJS | U.S. Department of Justice, Office of Justice Programs, Bureau of Justice Statistics |
| CEO | chief executive officer |
| CPA | certified public accountant |
| DOJ | U.S. Department of Justice |
| DPA | deferred-prosecution agreement |
| EOUSA | Executive Office for United States Attorneys |
| EPA | U.S. Environmental Protection Agency |
| FCPA | Foreign Corrupt Practices Act |
| ISDC | Interagency Suspension and Debarment Committee |
| LIONS | Legal Information Office Network System |
| MPC | Model Penal Code |
| NPA | nonprosecution agreement |
| PACER | Public Access to Court Electronic Records |
| SEC | U.S. Securities and Exchange Commission |
| SOX | Sarbanes-Oxley Act |
| TRAC | Transactional Records Access Clearinghouse |

CHAPTER ONE

# Introduction

> Did you ever expect a corporation to have a conscience, when it has no soul to damn; no body to kick?—Lord Chancellor First Baron Edward Thurlow (1731–1806)[1]

> Some will rob you with a six-gun, and some with a fountain pen.—"Pretty Boy Floyd," by Woody Guthrie (1958)

What should be the role of the criminal law in controlling corporate and other organizational behavior?[2] Historically, the role of criminal law and punishment has been to deter undesirable behavior, provide retribution for those wronged, and incapacitate the wrongdoer. On the

---

1 Quoted in John C. Coffee, Jr., "'No Soul to Damn: No Body to Kick': An Unscandalized Inquiry into the Problem of Corporate Punishment," *Michigan Law Review*, Vol. 79, No. 3, January 1981, pp. 386–459. Probably because it so pithily expresses some of the challenges of regulating enterprises, this quotation has been used repeatedly (Samuel L. Buell, "The Blaming Function of Entity Criminal Liability," *Indiana Law Journal*, Vol. 81, 2006, pp. 473–537, p. 475, n. 8, citing two additional sources). John Poynder (*Literary Extracts from English and Other Works: Collected During Half a Century Together with Some Original Matter*, London: J. Hatchard and Son, 1844, p. 268) quotes the passage as "Corporations have neither bodies to be punished, nor souls to be condemned; they therefore do as they like." Another version of this quotation was published in Lady Saba Holland Holland (*Memoir of the Reverend Sydney Smith*, Sarah Austin, ed., New York: Harper and Bros., 1855, p. 376), which relates that Thurlow said, "Why, you never expected justice from a company, did you? They have neither a soul to lose, nor a body to kick."

2 Throughout this report, we refer to *corporate* and *organizational liability* interchangeably. We note that the underlying issues addressed apply to a variety of organizational forms other than corporations, e.g., partnerships.

one hand, it seems only natural to apply criminal sanctions when a problematic activity is taken to aid the organization's interests. It also seems natural to wish to punish the organization as though the organization itself is culpable and should be punished. On the other hand, Thurlow's frustration, expressed in the quotation above, is certainly understandable. Corporations are legal constructions, and many of our intuitions about crime and punishment apply uneasily to such creations and individuals' activities to further the corporation's interests.[3] In this report, we provide an overview of the use of criminal sanctions in the corporate context, including both criminal prosecutions of corporations and criminal prosecutions of individuals acting on behalf of firms.

Every first-year law student is taught that criminal liability ordinarily requires an *actus reus* (bad act) and *mens rea* (guilty state of mind), because the criminal law generally punishes morally blameworthy behavior. But the application of this general framework, and particularly the concept of *mens rea*, to corporations or other organizations is far from obvious. Whose intent should be considered? On the one hand, we must recognize that attributing intent to a corporation, a legal fiction, is an instance of anthropomorphizing an inanimate object. On the other hand, such anthropomorphism is common, and we often speak of a corporation acting as if it were a single being with plans, goals, and other mental states.[4]

Applying these concepts to individuals in this context is also complex. For example, the difference between legal and illegal behavior can turn on exceedingly subtle distinctions of mind. A legal trade becomes illegal if and only if the government can prove *an intent* to defraud the

---

[3] For early critics of the anthropomorphization of the corporation, see Nathanial Lindley ("On the Principles Which Govern the Criminal and Civil Responsibilities of Corporations [March 30, 1857]," in *Juridical Society Papers*, Vol. 2, March 30, 1857, pp. 34–35) and Frederick Pollock ("Has the Common Law Received the Fiction Theory of Corporations?" *Law Quarterly Review*, Vol. 27, No. 2, 1911, pp. 219–235).

[4] For example, a recent headline in the *New York Times* reads, "E-Mails Imply JPMorgan Knew Some Mortgage Deals Were Bad" (Jessica Silver-Greenberg, "E-Mails Imply JPMorgan Knew Some Mortgage Deals Were Bad," *New York Times DealBook*, February 6, 2013, p. B1).

counterparty. Defining criminal activity in an area in which authorities must untangle aggressive but legal business behavior from illegal behavior is difficult.[5]

Recently, critics have argued that corporate behavior has been overcriminalized. On the most general level, these critics argue that criminal law is being overused as a tool to create incentives for good corporate behavior. This argument can encompass more-specific criticisms, including the number of criminal statutes, the fact that many criminal prohibitions are created by agencies rather than by Congress, by overly aggressive prosecutorial tactics, by the use of criminal rather than civil sanctions, and by too many criminal prosecutions overall. For example, some critics have noted the huge growth in the number of federal criminal statutes.[6] Others have noted with concern that many regulations that were enacted not by Congress but by federal agencies carry criminal penalties.[7] Others note the passage of statutes specifically targeting corporate behavior, such as the Sarbanes-Oxley Act of 2002 (SOX) and the Dodd-Frank Wall Street Reform and Consumer Protection Act,[8] and raise the potential unfairness of imposing criminal liability on individuals and organizations who did not have any criminal intention.[9]

On the other hand, others point out that very few corporate leaders have been prosecuted criminally, especially in the wake of the 2008 financial crisis. Wall Street executives have been described as "untouch-

---

[5] See Samuel L. Buell, "Is the White Collar Offender Privileged?" *Duke Law Journal*, Vol. 63, No. 4, January 2014, pp. 823–889.

[6] The Heritage Foundation, for example, claims that, between 1985 and 2008, Congress added 1,450 crimes to the federal criminal code. See Heritage Foundation, "Overcriminalization," *Solutions 2014*, undated; referenced February 28, 2014.

[7] William Shepherd, "A Country Overburdened by Too Many Laws," *Criminal Justice*, Vol. 28, No. 1, Spring 2013 (citing estimate of 300,000 violations in Title 18 [Crimes and Criminal Procedure] of the U.S. Code).

[8] Public Law 107-204, July 30, 2002; Public Law 111-203, July 21, 2010.

[9] David L. Douglass and Winifred M. Weitsen, "Overcriminalization of Corporate Acts: What Is a General Counsel to Do?" *In-House Defense Quarterly*, Winter 2013, pp. 26–31.

ables" for not facing prosecution.[10] Indeed, the Occupy Wall Street movement grew in part out of perceptions that large corporations face little scrutiny for actions that harmed millions.[11]

Generally, consternation about the role of criminal law in controlling behavior in the corporate context is not a new set of concerns. Thurlow's observation quoted above was only the first and most famous of many statements about the odd fit between the personal culpability that normally attends a criminal sanction and the literal impersonality of the corporation. A vast literature has accumulated on the fairness and wisdom of employing criminal liability against business organizations, and policymakers have long struggled to assess the wisdom and fairness of applying the criminal law, which developed to address individual wrongdoing, to corporate entities.[12]

Unfortunately, existing empirical research in this area provides limited guidance to policymakers. Past studies have focused on particular types of prosecutions, such as antitrust or Foreign Corrupt Practices Act (FCPA). As a result, it was difficult to draw any conclusions about the overall picture of the use of criminal liability. We draw on this research in our own analysis and review the available data from

---

[10] A PBS Frontline program titled *The Untouchables* describes the lack of prosecutions from the U.S. Department of Justice (DOJ) following the 2008 financial crisis (Jeff Connaughton, *The Payoff: Why Wall Street Always Wins*, Westport, Conn.: Prospecta Press, 2012; "Going Soft on Corporate Crime," *New York Times*, editorial, April 10, 2008; Matt Taibbi, "Gangster Bankers: Too Big to Jail," *Rolling Stone*, February 14, 2013).

[11] Occupy Wall Street, "About," undated; referenced June 3, 2013.

[12] See, e.g., Sanford H. Kadish, "Some Observations on the Use of Criminal Sanctions in Enforcing Economic Regulations," *University of Chicago Law Review*, Vol. 30, No. 3, Spring 1963, pp. 423–449, pp. 440–449; Norman Abrams, "Criminal Liability of Corporate Officers for Strict Liability Offenses—A Comment on *Dotterweich* and *Park*," *UCLA Law Review*, Vol. 28, No. 3, February 1981, pp. 463–477; James R. Elkins, "Corporations and the Criminal Law: An Uneasy Alliance," *Kentucky Law Journal*, Vol. 65, No. 1, 1976, pp. 73–129; W. B. Fisse, "The Social Policy of Corporate Criminal Responsibility," *Adelaide Law Review*, Vol. 6, No. 3, 1977–1978, pp. 361–412; Howard M. Friedman, "Some Reflections on the Corporation as Criminal Defendant," *Notre Dame Law Review*, Vol. 55, No. 2, December 1, 1979, pp. 173–202; Samuel R. Miller, "Corporate Criminal Liability: A Principle Extended to Its Limits," *Federal Bar Journal*, Vol. 38, No. 1, 1979, pp. 49–68; and V. S. Khanna, "Corporate Criminal Liability: What Purpose Does It Serve?" *Harvard Law Review*, Vol. 109, No. 7, May 1996, pp. 1477–1534.

multiple sources to get a broader picture of trends in this litigation (see Chapter Four).

## Overview of Corporate Criminal Liability

This report addresses the criminal liability of both corporations and individuals acting within these corporations. Corporations may be criminally liable for the crimes of their employees and agents. The agents and employees who commit the crimes may also face prosecution and punishment. As we discuss below, criminal statutes, Justice Department policies, and the Federal Sentencing Guidelines affect the circumstances under which agents, employees, and corporations are prosecuted and punished.

Criminal liability for the corporation itself is confined to offenses committed by the corporation's officers, employees, or agents within the scope of their employment and at least in part for the benefit of the corporation.[13] Whether an activity falls within the individual's scope of authority is determined by whether the individual engages in activities "on the corporation's behalf in performance of [his or her] general line of work. . . . [T]hose acts must be motivated, at least in part, by an intent to benefit the corporation."[14] Notably, if this standard is met, the corporation will be liable even if it expressly directed its agent not to commit the offense or offenses.[15]

Individual criminal liability exists for crimes that individual corporate employee, agents, or officers commit. But it also extends to crimes that individuals conspire with others to commit and for the

---

13 *United States v. Singh*, 518 F.3d 236, 249–250 (4th Cir. 2008):

> [A] corporation accused is liable for the criminal acts of its employees and agents acting within the scope of their employment for the benefit of the corporation and such liability arises if the employee or agent acted for his own benefit as well as that of his employer.

14 *United States v. Agosto-Vega*, 617 F.3d 541, 552–553 (1st Cir. 2010) ("[t]he test is whether the agent is performing acts of the kind which he is authorized to perform and those acts are motivated—at least in part—by an intent to benefit the corporation").

15 *United States v. Potter*, 463 F.3d 9, 26 (1st Cir. 2006); *United States v. Automated Medical Laboratories, Inc.*, 770 F.2d 399, 406 (4th Cir. 1985).

foreseeable crimes their coconspirators commit in furtherance of a common scheme. Accomplice liability extends to those who aid or abet another who commits a federal crime.[16] Finally, in the case of certain statutes, a responsible corporate officer may be criminally liable when he or she fails to prevent the commission of an offense, even when he or she has no knowledge of or participation in the criminal activity.[17]

The U.S. Department of Justice (DOJ) determines whether and what or whom to prosecute. Internal DOJ policy directives and the Federal Sentencing Guidelines for the judicial imposition of sentences upon conviction describe the criteria used to prosecute and the sentencing consequences. Typically, these include the strength of the case, the extent and history of misconduct, whether there is a compliance program, the corporation's cooperation with the investigation, the collateral consequences of the prosecution, and the extent of restitution, if any. As we discuss in more detail below, prosecutions of corporations rarely result in formal trials.

## Research Questions

The goal of this study was to synthesize what we know about the role of criminal law in controlling corporate behavior: Have we gone too far—or not far enough—in using the criminal law to punish and regu-

---

[16] From U.S. Code, Title 18, Crimes and Criminal Procedure, Part I, Crimes, Chapter 1, General Provisions, Section 2, Principals, 1976:

> (a) Whoever commits an offense against the United States or aids, abets, counsels, commands, induces or procures its commission, is punishable as a principal. (b) Whoever willfully causes an act to be done which if directly performed by him or another would be an offense against the United States, is punishable as a principal.

See, e.g., *United States v. Sain*, 141 F.3d 463 (3rd Cir. 1998) ("an individual who causes a corporation to commit a crime is criminally liable for the corporation's criminal conduct as an aider and abettor").

[17] See, e.g., *United States v. Dotterweich*, 320 U.S. 277 (1943); *United States v. Park*, 421 U.S. 658 (1975) (discussing such statutes).

late corporate behavior? To address these broad issues, we posed these specific questions:

- How did criminal liability, which historically focused on individual wrongdoing, come to be applied to a legal construction, the corporation? What lessons can we draw from that history?
- What are the recent developments in this area?
- What are the quantitative trends in criminal prosecutions of corporate activity over the past 25 years?
- How well is the system working? What policy reforms should be considered to address its shortcomings?

We offer no answer to the question as to whether corporate behavior is over- or undercriminalized. The question itself has little meaning without some normative theory as to the appropriate role for the criminal law. Although corporate criminal liability has grown enormously in the past 100 years, the number of prosecutions has actually declined in recent years. Collateral consequences of indictment and conviction (including reputational penalties and debarment from government contracts) that are outside prosecutors' control have made it harder for prosecutors to precisely titrate the effective punishment of corporations. The biggest recent development is the growth in deferred-prosecution agreements (DPAs) and nonprosecution agreements (NPAs), which have created their own complications.

## Research Approach and Sources of Data

In order to better understand the history of this issue, we first conducted legal research on the origins and development of criminal liability for corporations, vicarious liability for employers for the acts of their employees, and the evolution of the requirement of criminal intent. As noted above, criminal intent is particularly important in this area because many of the criminal offenses have relaxed the traditional requirements of criminal intent. To conduct this review, we examined the original legal cases in which these concepts developed and the considerable secondary literature. To address the recent developments in DOJ policies, we reviewed the relevant statements of policy issued by DOJ and the secondary literature.

Unfortunately, there is no single source of authoritative data on criminal prosecutions in this context. As a result, we drew from five primary sources of data from federal courts and agencies on the enforcement of laws that govern corporate behavior, which are briefly described here.

### *Federal Court Cases: Integrated Data Base*

This database provides data on all federal criminal, civil, and appellate cases for a given year.[18] In particular, this study used data from 2004 to 2008 from both criminal and civil cases.

#### Criminal-Case Data

The Administrative Office of the United States Courts collects these data from each of the 94 federal district courts.

The data for criminal cases contain information recording the district in which a case was filed; dates, including filing and termination; the federal circuit that has jurisdiction over the matter; and docket numbers. Each case entry identifies up to five filing offenses, which include the title and section of the U.S. Code in dispute. Furthermore, the data identify up to five sections of U.S. Code under which the case was terminated and sentencing information, such as the disposition type, prison and probation time, and criminal fines. The unit of analysis for these data is the defendant, who can appear in multiple cases. It is important to note that the original data identified all defendants' identities. However, the Urban Institute, in its responsibility for the the National Archives of Criminal Justice Data, the designated data repository, has stripped the identities of all defendants.[19] Thus, it is

[18] Federal Judicial Center, *Federal Court Cases: Integrated Data Base*, Ann Arbor, Mich.: Inter-university Consortium for Political and Social Research, 2011.

[19] A description of the data is available from U.S. Department of Justice, Office of Justice Programs, Bureau of Justice Statistics (BJS), *Federal Justice Statistics Program: Defendants in Federal Criminal Cases Filed in District Court, 2009*, Ann Arbor, Mich.: Inter-university Consortium for Political and Social Research, June 3, 2011ff.

impossible using these particular data to identify whether a defendant is an individual or a corporation.

### Civil-Case Data

The civil-case data contain similar information to that in the criminal cases, such as the district in which the dispute was disposed, the controlling circuit, and docket numbers. Also listed are both the plaintiffs' and the defendants' identities. Additionally, the relevant titles and sections of the U.S. Code are included, as well as the judgment rendered, the amount of damages awarded, and the disposition type. The unit of analysis is the individual civil court case.

### Executive Office for United States Attorneys Data

The Executive Office for United States Attorneys (EOUSA) compiles data on suspects involved in federal criminal matters, as well as charges filed against defendants by U.S. Attorneys. These data come from the U.S. Attorneys' Central System File and Legal Information Office Network System (LIONS) and are compiled and processed by the Urban Institute.[20] These data identify the section of U.S. Code under which a suspect was charged, the type of crime alleged, and incarceration and probation length. The unit of analysis for these data is the federal criminal matter in dispute. Thus, a suspect or defendant can appear in multiple cases. Additionally, these data are not as extensive as the data from the *Federal Court Cases: Integrated Data Base* because they are more focused on suspects involved in criminal matters and cases brought by U.S. Attorneys during their initial filing. As a result, the data from EOUSA contain limited sentencing information compared with other data used in this study. As in other data used in this study involving criminal matters, defendants' identities are sanitized, making it impossible to determine whether any defendant was an individual or a firm.

---

[20] A description of the data is available at BJS, *Federal Justice Statistics Program: Defendants Charged in Criminal Cases Filed in District Court, 2009*, Ann Arbor, Mich.: Inter-university Consortium for Political and Social Research, June 3, 2011ee.

## U.S. Sentencing Commission Data on Corporations Sentenced in Federal Courts

The U.S. Sentencing Commission is responsible for collecting data on all corporations sentenced under Chapter 8 of the Federal Sentencing Guidelines. Chapter 8 of the guidelines applies sentencing standards to all organizations convicted in a federal court of a class A misdemeanor or felony.[21] The Sentencing Commission data's unit of analysis is an individual corporation as a defendant. The data include a wide range of information, such as company size by number of employees, up to five federal statutes under which the firm was convicted, whether any individuals related to the matter were convicted alongside the firm, and the industry in which the firm operated.[22] Unfortunately, the data collected by the Sentencing Commission are incomplete and thus not a full representation of all federal criminal cases involving organizations. Several studies have noted important omissions of large companies that were not included in the Sentencing Commission's data sets.[23] There are several possible explanations for the missing data in the data sets. First, the Sentencing Commission relies on self-reported data from the federal courts. A court clerk or administrator could simply forget to record and submit information. If a court fails to submit the information by a deadline, the information may or may not be added retroactively. The 2009 Sentencing Commission annual report noted that case information was reported months or even years after adjudication.[24]

Second, not all crimes of which an organization can be convicted are sentenced under Chapter 8. Environmental crimes are sentenced

---

[21] U.S. Sentencing Commission, *2012 USSC Guidelines Manual*, 2012, § 8A1.1.

[22] Although the Sentencing Commission has collected data on corporations sentenced in federal courts since the late 1980s, this study used only Sentencing Commission data from 1994 to 2008. Data prior to 1994 did not provide the information necessary to conduct a coherent analysis for the period from the late 1980s to 2010.

[23] Cindy R. Alexander, Jennifer Arlen, and Mark A. Cohen, "Regulating Corporate Criminal Sanctions: Federal Guidelines and the Sentencing of Public Firms," *Journal of Law and Economics*, Vol. 42, No. S1, April 1999, pp. 393–422, p. 402; Brandon L. Garrett, "Globalized Corporate Prosecutions," *Virginia Law Review*, Vol. 97, No. 8, December 2011, pp. 1775–1876, pp. 1807–1808.

[24] U.S. Sentencing Commission, *2009 Annual Report*, c. 2009, p. 33.

under a different chapter of the guidelines. Although Chapter 8 applies to any organization convicted of a felony or class A misdemeanor, human error can lead to a misapplication of the guidelines. This creates the potential for organizations convicted of environmental crimes (or other crimes under different chapters) to be reported in data sets other than those used for recording information on organizations sentenced.

Researchers have attempted to overcome these limitations by supplementing the data provided by the Sentencing Commission. Cindy Alexander, Arlen, and Cohen bolstered the Sentencing Commission data with their own by searching publicly available sources, such as U.S. Securities and Exchange Commission (SEC) filing reports, *Wall Street Journal* index, Westlaw, LexisNexis, and Corporate Affiliations for public companies involved in prosecution.[25] For the period between 1988 and 1996, they found 243 sentences of publicly traded firms, whereas the Sentencing Commission data reported only 80.[26] However, they experienced limited success with combining the data, given the Sentencing Commission's failure to provide suitable information that can be used to identify individual cases.[27]

## TRACFED

This data set is compiled by the Transactional Records Access Clearinghouse (TRAC), a research center at Syracuse University. TRACFED is an online data warehouse that contains data on federal prosecutions similar to what the EOUSA data provide. TRACFED receives its information from the U.S. government through access guaranteed by the Freedom of Information Act.[28] Like EOUSA data, prosecution data are made available to TRACFED from the U.S. Attorneys' Central System File and LIONS. Unlike the data sets from EOUSA, which are processed by the Urban Institute, these cases are processed and made

---

25 C. Alexander, Arlen, and Cohen, 1999, p. 403.

26 See C. Alexander, Arlen, and Cohen, 1999.

27 C. Alexander, Arlen, and Cohen, 1999.

28 TRAC, "The Quick-Start Guide to TRAC and TRACFED," undated (c); referenced November 28, 2012; Public Law 89-487, amending § 3 of the Administrative Procedure Act, July 4, 1966.

available through TRAC. This difference can be important because the organizations most likely employ different methods for coding and categorizing the information into relational variables. TRAC, however, appears to have employed additional quality-control mechanisms and has pursued litigation to obtain defendant identifiers.[29]

### Garrett Database of Convicted Corporations

In response to the flaws of the Sentencing Commission data, Garrett compiled his own data on corporations convicted in federal courts between 2001 and 2010. His data include information similar to the Sentencing Commission data, such as firm size, the type of criminal dispute, and criminal fines. At the time of this study, his data consisted of 1,011 publicly reported convictions of corporations. Garrett obtained these data by searching plea agreements, docket sheets, SEC filings, press releases, Public Access to Court Electronic Records (PACER), Westlaw, and DOJ websites.[30] Because these data come from public sources, his data are skewed toward publicly traded firms, which tend to be large. In contrast, the Sentencing Commission data contain more information on smaller, non–publicly traded firms.

### Garrett Data on Deferred-Prosecution and Nonprosecution Agreements

In addition to compiling data on convicted corporations, Garrett compiled data on DPAs and NPAs between firms and DOJ. This data set contains such information as the date in which an agreement was entered and the terms of the agreement—such as whether an independent monitor was appointed and whether the firm paid any fines,

[29] TRAC, "About the Data: Judging the Quality of Government Data," undated (b); referenced November 29, 2012. TRAC subjects the data to systematic tests to ensure quality. Any discrepancies are brought to the attention of the supplying government agency. If a discrepancy cannot be resolved, the data are flagged to alert the user. A federal judge ordered DOJ to disclose information containing the name of the defendant corporation to TRAC (TRAC, "Department of Justice Ordered to Release Additional Information," press release, September 13, 2006; referenced November 29, 2012).

[30] Garrett, 2011, pp. 1871–1874.

including penalties and restitution. This was compiled from the same publicly available sources.

## Organization of This Report

In the next chapter, we provide a brief history of the evolution of criminal law as applied to corporations and their directors. We then turn to developments of the past 25 years, focusing on the passage of the Federal Sentencing Guidelines and how it changed the role of criminal law in controlling corporate behavior (Chapter Three). We also describe the case of Arthur Andersen and its effects on the rise of DPAs and NPAs as substitutes for the conventional criminal process. In Chapter Four, we review the empirical evidence on trends in prosecutions of corporations and corporate directors. Although the absence of a definitive data source reduces our ability to draw strong conclusions, a consistent story of declining formal prosecutions accompanied by a rise in DPAs and NPAs emerges from several sources of data. In our concluding chapter, we propose several recommendations for policymakers, prosecutors, and judges that emerge from our analysis.

CHAPTER TWO

# How Did Criminal Law Come to Be Applied to Corporate Behavior, and What Lessons Can We Draw from That History?

Some critics argue that it is unfair to shareholders and to corporate executives for criminal sanctions to be leveled against a corporation or a director without any proof of moral culpability or criminal intent on their part.[1] For shareholders, the argument of unfairness is that they are blameless for the actions of difficult-to-control wrongdoers within the corporation, and a similar argument can be raised for directors. Given the historical centrality of proof of criminal intent in the history of Anglo-American criminal law, its absence in this context is striking. A review of the relevant legal history is therefore helpful to understand how the current regime developed.[2]

This chapter explains how criminal liability expanded to include both corporate entities and corporate actors. We address three closely related shifts in the law that are important to understand the current status of criminal law in controlling corporations: (1) the emergence of criminal responsibility for corporations, (2) the development of vicarious criminal liability, and (3) the evolution of the requirement of *mens rea*, or criminal intent. Each of these developments was necessary for

[1] For example, Marc A. Levin, "At the State Level, So-Called Crimes Are Here, There, Everywhere," *Criminal Justice*, Vol. 28, No. 1, Spring 2013, pp. 4–9.

[2] Roman law addressed the problem of criminal behavior on the part of corporations by simply discouraging corporations. Noting that Trajan refused to incorporate even a small company of firefighters, Edward Gibbon (*The Decline and Fall of the Roman Empire*, Vol. 2: *Chapters XVI–XXV*, New York: Alfred A. Knopf, 1993, p. 10) noted, "Roman policy viewed with the utmost jealousy and distrust any association among its subjects; and that the privileges of private corporations, though formed for the most harmless or beneficial purposes, were bestowed with a very sparing hand."

the emergence of the current regime of criminal liability for corporate actions. The overall story that emerges is one of expanding corporate criminal liability and a shift away from criminal intent as being a prerequisite to criminal liability. This shift is usually justified on pragmatic grounds. We also see that criminal liability for both corporations and individuals without a requirement of criminal intent has a similarly long history.

## Emergence of Corporate Criminal Liability

Although, historically, corporations could be civilly liable,[3] they could not be criminally liable. As early as 1612, in the *Case of Sutton's Hospital*, it was noted that corporations "cannot commit treason, nor be outlawed, nor excommunicate, for they have no souls, neither can they appear in person, but by attorney."[4] The conventional authority for the ban on corporate criminal liability is Lord Chief Justice John Holt in 1701, to whom the following was ascribed: "A corporation is not indictable but the particular members of it are."[5] William Blackstone cited this as an authoritative statement of English law.[6]

The first steps toward criminal liability of corporations probably occurred in the 18th century, when governmental units were found vicariously liable for failing to maintain public conveniences and subject to fines.[7] By the 19th century, corporations were criminally liable

[3] See generally Kathleen F. Brickey, "Corporate Criminal Accountability: A Brief History and an Observation," *Washington University Law Quarterly*, Vol. 60, No. 2, 1982a, pp. 393–423, pp. 401–402, discussing development of corporate civil liability.

[4] *Case of Sutton's Hospital*, 77 Eng. Rep. 960, 973 (K.B. 1612).

[5] Anonymous, 88 Eng. Rep. 1518 (K.B. 1701). However, no fact, party, the nature of the dispute, or other information has survived to provide any context for this statement.

[6] William Blackstone, *Commentaries on the Laws of England*, 1765, p. 476 ("A corporation cannot commit treason, or felony, or other crime, in its corporate capacity: though its members may in their individual capacities").

[7] For example, *The King v. Inhabitants of Clifton*, 101 Eng. Rep. 280 (K.B. 1794).

for these *inactions*.[8] But the question of whether a corporation could be held liable for *actions* that were directly inconsistent with its charter remained unresolved until *Regina v. Great North of England R. Co.*[9] In this case, employees of the railway cut through an existing highway and left it covered with debris. These actions directly violated the charter of the railway. The court held that the distinction between wrongful acts (for which corporations were exempt) and wrongful omissions (for which they could be held criminally liable) showed a "startling incongruity"[10] and therefore found the railway criminally liable for this action.

Nonetheless, the court made it clear that corporations could not be held vicariously criminally liable for "acts of immorality," which "plainly derive their character from the corrupted mind of the person committing them. . . ."[11] For approximately the next 50 years, criminal prosecutions of corporations in England focused on offenses that did not require intentionality. After the turn of the century, however, even offenses that required a specific mental state were applied to corporations.[12]

### Immunity from Crimes Requiring Intent

In the United States, the road to corporate criminal liability began with public-nuisance actions. As in England, *inaction* by the corporation was first targeted.[13] However, this distinction between action and

---

8 *The Queen v. Birmingham & Gloucester Ry.*, 114 Eng. Rep. 492 (Q.B. 1842) (railroad liable for ignoring statute directing it to construct arches over railway).

9 115 Eng. Rep. 1294 (Q.B. 1846) (Lord Denman).

10 *Regina*, 115 Eng. Rep. at 1298.

11 *Regina*, 115 Eng. Rep. at 1298.

12 See, e.g., *Chuter v. Freeth & Pocock Ltd.*, 2 K.B. 832 (1911) (corporation properly convicted for providing false warranty under sale-of-food-and-drugs act, despite a requirement under the relevant statute that the issuer know that the warranty is false).

13 See, e.g., *People v. Corporation*, 11 Wend. 539 (N.Y. Sup. Ct. 1834) (failure to maintain polluted river basin); *Commonwealth v. Hancock Free Bridge Corp.*, 68 Mass. 58 (1854) (poorly maintained roadway); *State v. Morris Canal & Banking Co.*, 22 N.J.L. 537 (1850) (unmaintained bridge); and *State v. Corporation of Shelbyville*, 36 Tenn. 176 (1856) (failure to diminish odors from slaughterhouse).

inaction was rejected in *State v. Morris & E. R. Co.*[14] The court noted that there was no logical distinction as to why a corporation might be found criminally liable of inaction but not action: "why for neglect of duty, and not for violation of law?"[15]

The court also squarely rejected the argument that a corporation could not be held liable for actions taken outside its corporate charter:

> According to the doctrine contended for, if they do an act within the scope of their corporate powers it is legal, and they are not answerable for the consequences. If the act be not within the range of their corporate powers, they had no right to do it; it was not one of the objects for which they were incorporated, and therefore is no act of the corporation at all. This doctrine leads to absolute impunity for every species of wrong, and can never be sanctioned by any court of justice.[16]

The court also addressed an argument with a contemporary ring[17]—the suggestion that the better policy was to seek to hold individual defendants liable for illegal activities rather than indict the corporation itself:

> It is said, again, that the individuals who concur in making the order or in doing the work are individually responsible. And so is every servant or agent by whose agency a *tort* is committed, but it has never been supposed that the principal is therefore exempt from liability. On the contrary, the principle and the policy of the law has ever been to look to the principal rather than to the mere agent; and in the case of corporations, it is the clear dictate of sound law not only, but of public policy, to look rather to the corporation at whose instance and for whose benefit the wrong is perpetrated, than to the individual directors by whose order the

---

[14] 23 N.J.L. 360 (1852).

[15] *Morris & E. R.*, 23 N.J.L. at 369.

[16] *Morris & E. R.*, 23 N.J.L. at 369 (quoting Binney's argument in *The Chestnut Hill Turnpike Co. v. Rutter*, 4 Serg. & Rawl. 6, 12 [Pa. 1818]).

[17] See Buell, 2014, p. 40, n. 6 (noting that focusing on individual wrongdoers and bad apples "crowd[s] out [arguments] about system failure").

> wrong was done, who may be entirely unknown, or to the laborers by whom the work was performed, who, in a great majority of cases, would be alike unknown and irresponsible.[18]

The court found that, for instrumental policy reasons, because it would be difficult to identify the responsible directors or workers, the corporation itself should be criminally liable.

Interestingly, the court also suggested that it is fairer, in the context of nuisance abatement, for the corporation itself, rather than individuals, to be a party:

> If the rights of the corporation are to be concluded by the judgment, as in the present case, a valuable building, erected by the company at great cost for their own convenience, is to be ordered to be torn down as an encroachment upon the highway, there is peculiar propriety in making the corporation itself a party, and giving it an opportunity of being heard in defense. To condemn the property of the corporation to destruction upon an indictment against an irresponsible individual who was employed in the construction of the work, but who has no interest in the company, and who perhaps is hostile to its interests, savors strongly of the injustice of condemning them unheard.[19]

The idea that the corporation itself might have an independent stake and standing in the outcome of proceedings against an individual is not an argument often made today.

After *State v. Morris & E. R. Co.* and *Commonwealth v. Proprietors of New Bedford Bridge*,[20] another prominent case rejecting the distinction between action and inaction, vicarious criminal liability for corporations was fairly well established in this country. Subsequent cases found corporations criminally liable for such varied criminal offenses as

---

[18] *Morris & E. R.*, 23 N.J.L. at 369.

[19] *Morris & E. R.*, 23 N.J.L. at 370.

[20] 68 Mass. 339 (1854).

the unauthorized practice of medicine, breaking the Sabbath, gaming on a fairground, usury, and furnishing liquor to minors.[21]

In contrast, however, corporations remained immune from prosecution for crimes requiring intent. Three justifications for this immunity were forwarded. The first was that corporations could not be subject to corporeal punishment. The felonies of this era often carried a punishment of death or dismemberment in most jurisdictions. Because it was impossible to physically punish corporations, corporations could not be found guilty of crimes that carried such punishments. However, as more crimes were deemed felonies, this rule was criticized. Bishop noted that, although a "corporation cannot be hung: yet there is no reason why it may not be fined, or suffer the loss of its franchise, for the same act which would subject an individual to the gallows."[22]

Second, some argued that, because the purpose of the corporation was to engage in legal actions, some activities were so far outside the proper corporate purpose that prosecuting a corporation for a crime requiring intent would be contrary to principal-agent law. So, for example, one court adopted a continuum of *ultra vires* activity (that is, activity outside the corporation's charter):

> A corporation, especially as viewed from the standpoint of the criminal law, is an artificial creation of the law. . . . To determine what part and how much it covers, we look at its particular nature and objects, and the terms of the act of incorporation. Hence a corporation cannot, in its corporate capacity, commit a crime by an act in the fullest sense *ultra vires* and contrary to its nature. But within the sphere of its corporate capacity, and to an undefined extent beyond, whenever it assumes to act as a corporation, it has the same capabilities of criminal intent and of act—in other

---

21 *People v. John H. Woodbury Dermatological Institute*, 192 N.Y. 454 (1908); *State v. B. & O. R. R. Co.*, 15 W.Va. 362 (1879); *Commonwealth v. Pulaski County Agricultural & Mechanical Ass'n*, 92 Ky. 197 (1891); *State v. First Nat'l Bank*, 2 S.D. 568 (1892); *Southern Express Co. v. State*, 1 Ga. App. 700 (1907).

22 Joel Prentiss Bishop, *Commentaries on the Criminal Law*, 3rd ed., 1865, § 506.

> words, of crime—as an individual man sustaining to the thing the like relations.[23]

Third, some argued that, because the corporation had "no soul," it could not have "actual wicked intent."[24] Accordingly, another distinction that arose in this era was between crimes that required specific intent and those that required a more generalized intent. One court explained the concept of corporate intent this way:

> If, for example, the invisible, intangible essence of air which we term a corporation can level mountains, fill up valleys, lay down iron tracks, and run railroad cars on them, it can also intend to do these acts, and can therein as well viciously as virtuously. The ordinary crimes, wherein only general evil, or the mere purpose to do the forbidden thing, suffices for the intent, are plainly within this doctrine.[25]

Interestingly, some individual defendants (prosecuted as individuals) attempted to argue that, because they were acting on behalf of a corporation, they could not personally be found criminally liable for acts taken to aid the corporation, arguing that the law should look to the principal rather than the agent.[26] However, this claim seems to have been universally rejected, with the courts generally finding that the individual defendants were using the corporations as instrumentalities for their individual acts.[27]

### Disappearance of Immunity for Crimes Requiring Intent

In the early 20th century, legal thinking shifted and allowed corporations to be found guilty even of criminal offenses that require intent.

---

[23] *United States v. Alaska Packers Asso.*, 1 Alaska 217, 220 (1901) (quoting Bishop).

[24] *First Nat'l Bank*, 2 S.D. at 571 (1892).

[25] *Alaska Packers Asso.*, 1 Alaska at 220 (1901).

[26] See, e.g., *Milbrath v. State*, 138 Wis. 354 (1909) and *United States v. MacAndrews & Forbes Co.*, 149 F. 823 (S.D.N.Y. 1906).

[27] *MacAndrews & Forbes Co.*, 149 F. 823 (1906).

In 1909, *New York Central R. Co. v. United States*,[28] the U.S. Supreme Court upheld criminal liability for corporations against arguments that doing so would be unfair to shareholders:

> It is contended that these provisions of the law are unconstitutional because Congress has no authority to impute to a corporation the commission of criminal offenses, or to subject a corporation to a criminal prosecution by reason of the things charged. The argument is that to thus punish the corporation is in reality to punish the innocent stockholders, and to deprive them of their property without opportunity to be heard, consequently without due process of law. And it is further contended that these provisions of the statute deprive the corporation of the presumption of innocence—a presumption which is part of due process in criminal prosecutions.[29]

The Court also considered the arguments that any criminal action committed by the corporation would be *ultra vires*:

> It is urged that, as there is no authority shown by the board of directors or the stockholders for the criminal acts of the agents of the company, in contracting for and giving rebates, they could not be lawfully charged against the corporation. As no action of the board of directors could legally authorize a crime, and as, indeed, the stockholders could not do so, the arguments come to this: That, owing to the nature and character of its organization and the extent of its power and authority, a corporation cannot commit a crime of the nature charged in this case.[30]

Although the Court acknowledged that "some of the earlier writers on common law held the law to be that a corporation could not commit a crime,"[31] it found that, under "the modern authority, univer-

---

[28] 212 U.S. 481 (1909).

[29] *New York Central R. Co.*, 212 U.S. 481 (1909).

[30] *New York Central R. Co.*, 212 U.S. 481 (1909).

[31] *New York Central R. Co.*, 212 U.S. 481 (1909), citing Blackstone (1765, chapter 18, § 12) ("A corporation cannot commit treason, or felony, or other crime in its corporate capacity,

sally, so far we know, it is the other way," i.e., finding vicarious criminal liability acceptable. Although the court noted that some classes of crime could not be committed by a corporation, it did not explain or develop this suggestion.

Other courts of this era addressed the lingering distinction between specific-intent crimes and general-intent crimes. Because it was possible for a corporation to be liable for an intentional tort, it seemed odd and inconsistent to find that corporations were immune from specific-intent crimes. The esteemed judge Learned Hand squarely addressed this issue in *United States v. Nearing*,[32] a case in which the defendants urged that a corporation could not be found guilty of conspiracy, a specific-intent crime:

> Finally, the defendants urge that a corporation cannot be guilty of the crime of conspiracy, or of any crime involving specific intent. This question simply turns upon how far the law has gone in imputing to a corporation the acts of its agents. . . . It is a question upon which the law has always tended towards larger and larger liability. . . . Now, there is no distinction in essence between the civil and the criminal liability of corporations, based upon the element of intent or wrongful purpose. Each is merely an imputation to the corporation of the mental condition of its agents. . . . That the criminal liability of a corporation is to be determined by the kinship of the act to the powers of the officials, who commit it is true enough, but neither the doctrine of *ultra vires*, nor the difficulty of imputing intent or motive, should be regarded any longer to determine the result.[33]

On Hand's reasoning, because corporations had long been found to have committed intentional torts, there was no reason they could not also be found to commit intentional crimes. For Hand, corporate criminal liability did not seem to provoke any difficult quasi-theological debates about the capacity of a legal fiction to have wicked intent—for

---

though its members may, in their distinct individual capacities").

[32] 252 F. 223, 231 (S.D.N.Y. 1918).

[33] *Nearing*, 252 F. 223 (S.D.N.Y. 1918).

him, it was a straightforward example of imputing to the principal the intent of the agent.

Another court found that, because a corporation was the creation of the legislature, the same legislature could subject it to criminal liability.[34] However, other commentators have disagreed with the suggestion that authorities in this era accepted vicarious criminal liability.[35]

When the midcentury Model Penal Code (MPC)[36] recognized vicarious corporate criminal liability, its reporters emphasized its pragmatic justifications and acknowledged the relative weakness of this justification. "In many cases . . . such penal provisions . . . form an integral part of the regulatory policy and are based on considerable pragmatic experience indicating their usefulness."[37] One reporter all but pined for a better justification: "It would be hoped that more could be pointed to in justification of placing the pecuniary burdens of criminal fines on the innocent than the difficulties of proving the guilt of the culpable individual."[38]

By the later decades of the 20th century, criminal liability for corporations was well established. Although some statutes specifically refer to punishing corporations directly, others specifically refer to corporations in the penalty section.[39] Still others indicate that acts and

---

[34] *MacAndrews & Forbes Co.*, 149 F. 823, 836 (1906).

[35] Glanville Llewellyn Williams, *Criminal Law: The General Part*, 2nd ed., London: Stevens, 1961, p. 853 (describing acceptance of vicarious liability as "a striking instance of judicial change in the law").

[36] American Law Institute, *Model Penal Code: Proposed Official Draft*, Philadelphia, Pa., 1962.

[37] American Law Institute, *Model Penal Code: Tentative Draft No. 4*, Philadelphia, Pa., 1955, p. 147, quoted in Gerhard O. W. Mueller, "*Mens Rea* and the Corporation: A Study of the Model Penal Code Position on Corporate Criminal Liability," *University of Pittsburgh Law Review*, Vol. 19, No. 1, Fall 1957, pp. 21–50, p. 27.

[38] Mueller, 1957.

[39] Examples of statutes that refer specifically to punishing corporations directly are U.S. Code, Title 15, Commerce and Trade, Chapter 1, Monopolies and Combinations in Restraint of Trade, Section 7, "Person" or "Persons" Defined, 1976; U.S. Code, Title 15, Commerce and Trade, Chapter 2A, Securities and Trust Indentures, Subchapter I, Domestic Securities, Section 77b, Definitions—Promotion of Efficiency, Competition, and Capi-

omissions of corporate agents within the scope of employment will be

---

tal Formation, 1976; U.S. Code, Title 15, Commerce and Trade, Chapter 2B, Securities Exchanges, Section 78c, Definitions and Application, 1976; U.S. Code, Title 21, Food and Drugs, Chapter 9, Federal Food, Drug, and Cosmetic Act, Subchapter II, Definitions, Section 321, Definitions—Generally, 1976; U.S. Code, Title 41, Public Contracts, Chapter 1, General Provisions, Section 52, Definitions, 1976.

Examples of statutes that refer to corporations in their penalty sections are U.S. Code, Title 12, Banks and Banking, Chapter 3, Federal Reserve System, Subchapter X, Powers and Duties of Member Banks, Section 378, Dealers in Securities Engaging in Banking Business—Individuals or Associations Engaging in Banking Business, Examinations and Reports, Penalties, 1976; U.S. Code, Title 15, Commerce and Trade, Chapter 15, Economic Recovery, Subchapter II, Commodity Credit Corporation, Section 714m, Crimes and Offenses, 1976; U.S. Code, Title 21, Food and Drugs, Chapter 12, Meat Inspection, Subchapter I, Inspection Requirements—Adulteration and Misbranding, Section 602, Congressional Statement of Findings, 1976; U.S. Code, Title 21, Food and Drugs, Chapter 12, Meat Inspection, Subchapter I, Inspection Requirements—Adulteration and Misbranding, Section 610, Prohibited Acts, 1976; U.S. Code, Title 21, Food and Drugs, Chapter 12, Meat Inspection, Subchapter I, Inspection Requirements—Adulteration and Misbranding, Section 611, Devices, Marks, Labels, and Certificates—Simulations, 1976; U.S. Code, Title 21, Food and Drugs, Chapter 4, Animals, Meats, and Meat and Dairy Products, Subchapter I, Examination of Animals, Meats, and Meat and Dairy Products, Section 88, 1976; U.S. Code, Title 21, Food and Drugs, Chapter 4, Animals, Meats, and Meat and Dairy Products, Subchapter I, Examination of Animals, Meats, and Meat and Dairy Products, Section 90, 1976; U.S. Code, Title 33, Navigation and Navigable Waters, Chapter 1, Navigable Waters Generally, Subchapter I, General Provisions, Section 1, Regulations by Secretary of the Army for Navigation of Waters Generally, 1976; U.S. Code, Title 33, Navigation and Navigable Waters, Chapter 1, Navigable Waters Generally, Subchapter I, General Provisions, Section 3, Regulations to Prevent Injuries from Target Practice, 1976; U.S. Code, Title 33, Navigation and Navigable Waters, Chapter 9, Protection of Navigable Waters and of Harbor and River Improvements Generally, Subchapter I, In General, Section 406, Penalty for Wrongful Construction of Bridges, Piers, etc.—Removal of Structures, 1976; U.S. Code, Title 33, Navigation and Navigable Waters, Chapter 9, Protection of Navigable Waters and of Harbor and River Improvements Generally, Subchapter I, In General, Section 411, Penalty for Wrongful Deposit of Refuse—Use of or Injury to Harbor Improvements, and Obstruction of Navigable Waters Generally, 1976; U.S. Code, Title 33, Navigation and Navigable Waters, Chapter 9, Protection of Navigable Waters and of Harbor and River Improvements Generally, Subchapter I, In General, Section 419, Regulation by Secretary Governing Transportation and Dumping of Dredgings, Refuse, etc., into Navigable Waters—Oyster Lands, Appropriations, 1976; U.S. Code, Title 33, Navigation and Navigable Waters, Chapter 9, Protection of Navigable Waters and of Harbor and River Improvements Generally, Subchapter III, New York Harbor, Harbor of Hampton Roads, and Harbor of Baltimore, Section 449, Disposition of Dredged Matter—Persons Liable, Penalty, 1976; U.S. Code, Title 33, Navigation and Navigable Waters, Chapter 12, River and Harbor Improvements Generally, Subchapter IV, Particular Work or Improvements, Section 602, Maintenance of Channel of South Pass of considered those of the corporation.[40]

## The Development of Vicarious Criminal Liability

A closely related legal concept to corporate criminal liability is vicarious criminal liability—that is, the liability of superiors for the actions of their employees. This is relevant today in the corporate context because various statutes create criminal penalties for directors of corporations for acts or inactions of employees of the corporation.

Originally, at common law, this concept (referred to as *respondeat superior*) did not apply to either civil or criminal cases—the act of the servant could not be imputed to the master unless the master directed the servant to engage in the wrongful action. However, beginning around 1700, the English courts begun to develop *respondeat superior* for torts.[41] But it was clear that this doctrine was (at least initially) limited to tort cases. As one English court put it, "It is a point not to be disputed, but that in criminal cases, the principal is not answerable for the act of the deputy, as he is in civil cases. . . ."[42]

The first cases to apply this doctrine in the criminal context were public-nuisance cases. Although these were criminal actions, perhaps their close relation to tort law made the application easier. This was also the first context in which vicarious corporate criminal liability devel-

Mississippi River, 1976; U.S. Code, Title 33, Navigation and Navigable Waters, Chapter 20, Pollution of the Sea by Oil, Section 1001, 1976.

[40] For example, U.S. Code, Title 7, Agriculture, Chapter 1, Commodity Exchanges, Section 4, 1976; U.S. Code, Title 7, Agriculture, Chapter 19, Cotton Statistics and Estimates, Section 473c-3, Liability of Principal for Act of Agent, 1976.

[41] For example, *Boson v. Sandford* was a case in which the plaintiffs urged that the ship owners were liable for the negligence of the ship captain. In finding for the plaintiffs, Holt explained, "The owners are liable in respect of the freight, and as employing the master; for whoever employs another is answerable for him, and undertakes for his care to all that make use of him" (90 Eng. Rep. 377, 638 [K.B. 1690]).

[42] *Rex v. Huggins*, 93 Eng. Rep. 915 (K.B. 1730).

oped.[43] In the 1834 case of *Rex v. Medley*,[44] for example, the directors and employees of Equitable Gas Company were indicted for polluting the Thames. The directors argued that, because they were not aware of the pollution, they could not be criminally liable. The judge rejected this claim and instructed the jury that the directors could be found criminally liable and that, "[i]f persons for their own advantage employ servants to conduct works, they must be answerable for what is done by those servants."[45] This rule was held to apply even in a context in which the owner specifically ordered his employees to comply with the law.[46]

In the United States, several courts found that vicarious liability was appropriate. In 1890, the Michigan Supreme Court upheld nuisance convictions of both the corporation and the corporate officers in *People v. Detroit Lead Works*.[47] The court explained,

> It is not necessary to conviction that they should have been actually engaged in work upon the premises. The work is carried on by employees. The directors and officers are the persons primarily responsible, and therefore the proper ones to be prosecuted. A fine can be collected against the defendant company, and therefore it is subject to prosecution.[48]

The Washington Supreme Court also addressed the issue of vicarious criminal liability in *State v. Constatine*.[49] In this case, a tavern owner was convicted of selling alcohol to a minor despite the fact that the owner was out of state at the time and had directed his bartenders not to do so. The court rejected his appeal, noting that, although

---

[43] See Brickey, 1982a.

[44] 172 Eng. Rep. 1246 (K.B. 1834).

[45] *Medley*, 172 Eng. Rep. at 1250.

[46] In 1866, in *The Queen v. Stephens*, the owner of a slate quarry was found liable for obstructing a river, which was accomplished by his employees, even when he specifically warned them not to do so (L.R. 1 Q.B. 702 [1866]).

[47] 82 Mich. 471, 737 (Mich. 1890).

[48] *Detroit Lead Works*, 82 Mich. at 479 (1890).

[49] 43 Wash. 102 (1906).

> it is undoubtedly a general rule of law that there can be no crime without a criminal intent, and that one man is not criminally responsible for the acts of another, even though such other be his agent or servant, unless something more than the mere relation of master and servant is shown, but there are many exceptions to the rule.[50]

Similarly, in 1912, vicarious criminal liability was also upheld in the case of *State v. Burnam*[51] for the manager of the Northwestern Dairy Company when a sealed bottle of milk had been watered down. The defendant argued that he lacked any knowledge of the diluted milk and "that his instructions were to keep the milk up to the standards fixed by law." The court rejected this defense and explained that the law was a "police regulation enacted for the protection of the public health, and the penalty is imposed without regard to any wrongful intention, in order to insure such diligence as will render a violation of the law practically impossible."[52]

The expansion of vicarious criminal liability for actions of employees, such as the expansion of criminal liability to corporations, was justified on pragmatic, rather than theoretical, grounds. Courts upheld these expansions on grounds that legislatures were justified in extending criminal penalties in order to improve public welfare.

---

[50] *Constatine*, 43 Wash at 104 (1906). See also *Carroll v. State*, 63 Md. 551, 3 A. 29 (1885):

> When the agent, as in this case, is set to do the very thing, which and which only, the principal's business contemplates, namely the dispensing of liquors to purchasers, the principal must be chargeable with the agent's violation of legal restriction on that business. His gains are increased, and he must bear the consequences. The fact that he has given orders not to sell to minors only shows a bona fide intent to obey the law, which all authorities say is immaterial in determining guilt.

[51] 71 Wash. 199, 219 (1912).

[52] *Burnam*, 71 Wash. at 200 (1912).

## Diminishing Relevance of Criminal Intent

A closely related issue is the centrality of *mens rea*, or criminal intent, to a criminal conviction and the question of whose mental state is relevant. If a culpable *mens rea* on the part of the defendant were strictly required, vicarious criminal liability of individual directors for acts taken by others would be impossible. Similarly, criminal liability of a corporation would be impossible. Our review of the case law shows that directors have long been found liable without any evidence of criminal intent on their part.

Criminal intent has been a central feature of Anglo-American criminal law for centuries. As Francis Sayre put it, writing in the *Harvard Law Review* in 1932, "For hundreds of years the books have repeated with unbroken cadence that *Actus non facit reum nisi mens sit rea*"[53]—"All crimes have their conception in a corrupt intent, and have their consummation and issuing in some particular fact." The influence of canon law brought a religious cast to the evaluation of the defendant's mental state:[54] "Under the pervasive influence of the Church, the teaching of the penitential books that punishment should be dependent upon moral guilt gave powerful impetus to this growth, for the very essence of moral guilt is a mental element."[55]

---

[53] Francis Bowes Sayre, "Mens Rea," *Harvard Law Review*, Vol. 45, 1932, p. 974, quoting Sir Edward Coke, *The Third Part of the Institutes of the Laws of England: Concerning High Treason, and Other Pleas of the Crown, and Criminall Causes*, London: M. Flesher, 1641, pp. 6, 107; see also Francis Bacon, *The Elements of the Common Lawes of England: Branched into a Double Trial*, Clark, N.J.: Lawbook Exchange Ltd., 2003 ("All crimes have their conception in a corrupt intent, and have their consummation and issuing in some particular fact").

[54] Sayre, 1932, pp. 983–984.

[55] Sayre, 1932, p. 988; see also Deborah W. Denno, "Criminal Law in a Post-Freudian World," *University of Illinois Law Review*, Vol. 2005, 2005, pp. 601–774, p. 612. Though even in Bracton, often cited for evidence of the centrality of *mens rea* in Anglo-American criminal law, one can find criminal liability absent evil intent; see, e.g., Henry de Bracton, *On the Laws and Customs of England*, George E. Woodbine, ed., Samuel E. Thorne, trans., Cambridge: Belknap Press of Harvard University Press, 1968, p. 384. See also Samuel H. Pillsbury, "Evil and the Law of Murder," *University of California Davis Law Review*, Vol. 24, No. 2, Winter 1990, pp. 437–488, pp. 460–463.

This emphasis on evil moral intent fits awkwardly with organizational criminal liability. What does it mean for an organization to have a morally culpable mental state? What indicia of evil or sin would even an omniscient fact finder seek?

In the United States, exceptions to the general rule requiring intent can be found as early as the mid–19th century. For example, in *Barnes v. State*, the Connecticut Supreme Court upheld a conviction for selling liquor to a habitual drunkard, absent evidence that the tavern keeper was aware of the fact.[56] And for the Michigan Supreme Court, Chief Justice Thomas M. Cooley noted,

> I agree that as a rule there can be no crime without a criminal intent, but this is not by any means a universal rule. . . . Many statutes which are in the nature of police regulations as this is, impose criminal penalties irrespective of any intent to violate them, the purpose being to require a degree of diligence for the protection of the public which shall render violation impossible.[57]

In his famed 1881 treatise, *The Common Law*, Oliver Wendell Holmes observed that courts have often imposed strict liability absent *mens rea* and used criminal offenses for purposes other than moral blameworthiness—"theory and fact agree in frequently punishing those who have been guilty of no moral wrong."[58] He summarized criminal liability as follows:

> In the characteristic type of substantive crime acts are rendered criminal because they are done under circumstances in which they will probably cause some harm which the law seeks to prevent. The test of criminality in such cases is the degree of danger

---

[56] *Barnes v. State*, 19 Conn. 398 (1849). See also *Commonwealth v. Farren*, 91 Mass. 489 (1864) (no knowledge required for crime of selling adulterated milk).

[57] *People v. Roby*, 52 Mich. 577, 18 N.W. 365, 366 (1884). Justice Cooley also noted in passing that one can be guilty of manslaughter, a felony, though "his only fault is gross negligence" (52 Mich. 577).

[58] Oliver Wendell Holmes, Jr., *The Common Law*, Boston, Mass.: Little, Brown, and Company, 1881, pp. 44–45; see also *Roby*, 52 Mich. at 51–58 (noting ways in which even the traditional crime of murder ignores the specifics of individual culpability).

> shown by experience to attend that act under those circumstances. In such cases, the *mens rea*, or actual wickedness of the party, is wholly unnecessary, and all reference to the state of his consciousness is misleading if it means anything more than that the circumstances in connection with which the tendency of his act is judged are the circumstances known to him.[59]

In Holmes's view, criminal intent was not at all necessary to criminal liability because the primary goal of the criminal law was to regulate conduct—not punish morally culpable conduct.[60] This understanding of criminal liability is consistent with the 19th century's steady expansion of criminal liability to corporations.

By the beginning of the 20th century, New York had attached criminal fines to regulations regarding conditions of tenement houses. Landlords protested and argued that criminal intent was required to convict them of a criminal offense. Judge Benjamin N. Cardozo rejected this argument, explaining,

> The defendant asks us to test the meaning of this statute by standards applicable to statutes that govern infamous crimes. . . . The element of conscious wrongdoing, the guilty mind accompanying the guilty act, is associated with the concept of crimes that are punished as infamous.[61]

Because the violation of a regulation did not qualify as an "infamous crime," it was not problematic to convict a defendant without proof of intent.

In a subsequent case, Cardozo extended this precedent to employers who were convicted of violating labor laws. But he also sounded a

---

59 Holmes, 1881, p. 75.

60 Among other examples, he pointed out that, in Macauley's draft of the Indian Penal Code (Act 45 of 1860), breaches of contract for the carriage of passengers were made criminal—not because the carriers were morally blameworthy but because harm could come to the passengers and civil remedies were ineffective (because the carriers were too poor to sue) (Holmes, 1881, p. 40); see also Holmes, 1881, p. 50 ("[T]he tests of [criminal] liability are external, and independent of the degree of evil in the particular person's motives or intentions").

61 *Tenement House Dep't v. McDevitt*, 109 N.E. 88, 90 (N.Y. 1915).

note of caution: "[W]e are not to be understood as sustaining to a like length the power to imprison. We leave that question open."[62]

In 1923, the Washington Supreme Court faced a question of the centrality of intent in *State v. Lindberg*.[63] In that case, a statute made it a felony for a banker to borrow funds from his own bank in excess of a certain amount without following certain procedures. Another official of the bank had assured the defendant banker that the relevant funds had come from another bank. The trial court excluded this testimony and ruled that the statute did not include any intent requirement. The Washington Supreme Court affirmed the conviction and explained,

> In these cases there is a voluntary act which the party does at his peril, and he is not to be excused either by ignorance of the law or ignorance of the fact. Either kind of ignorance implies a fault, and it must be assumed that with due diligence the true character of the act could have been ascertained.[64]

The U.S. Supreme Court addressed these issues in 1943 in *Dotterweich*.[65] The Federal Food, Drug, and Cosmetic Act of 1938 prohibited "the introduction or delivery for introduction into interstate commerce of any . . . drug . . . that is adulterated or misbranded." The defendant, Dotterweich, was the president of Buffalo Pharmacal Company and was found guilty under the act. The Court of Appeals had reversed his conviction on the grounds that only the corporation was the "person" subject to prosecution and that Dotterweich could not be individually criminally liable.

However, the Supreme Court reinstated his conviction, explaining,

> The prosecution to which Dotterweich was subjected is based on a now familiar type of legislation whereby penalties serve as effective means of regulation. Such legislation dispenses with the con-

---

62 *People ex rel. Price v. Sheffield Farms-Slawson-Decker Co.*, 121 N.E. 474, 476 (Ct. App. N.Y. 1918).

63 125 Wash. 51 (1923).

64 *Lindberg*, 125 Wash. at 64 (1923), citing *State v. Nicolls*, 61 Wash. 142 (1910).

65 320 U.S. 277 (1943).

> ventional requirement for criminal conduct—awareness of some wrongdoing. In the interest of the larger good it puts the burden of acting at hazard upon a person otherwise innocent but standing in responsible relation to a public danger.[66]

Although the court acknowledges that "hardship there doubtless may be under a statute which thus penalizes the transaction though consciousness of wrongdoing be totally wanting," it found that Congress balanced this hardship against that of the "innocent public who are wholly helpless."[67]

The dissent, in contrast, noted that "it is a fundamental principle of Anglo-Saxon jurisprudence that guilt is personal and that it ought not lightly to be imputed to a citizen who, like the respondent, has no evil intention or consciousness of wrongdoing."[68] Absent clarity in the statute, the dissent argued that it should not find vicarious liability of a corporate officer for crimes committed by the corporation.

Some commentators vigorously protested the Court's decision upholding criminal liability absent proof of intent. Sayre argued that "[t]o inflict substantial punishment upon one who is morally entirely innocent, who caused injury through reasonable mistake or pure accident, would so outrage the feelings of the community as to nullify its own enforcement."[69] Similarly, Jerome Hall argued that strict liability in the criminal law was a grievous mistake:

> It is impossible to defend strict liability in terms of or by reference to the only criteria that are available to evaluate the influence of legal controls on human behavior. What then remains is the myth that through devious, yet unknown ways, some good comes from strict liability in "penal" law.[70]

---

[66] *Dotterweich*, 320 U.S. at 280–281.

[67] *Dotterweich*, 320 U.S. at 284.

[68] *Dotterweich*, 320 U.S. at 286.

[69] Francis Bowes Sayre, "Public Welfare Offenses," *Columbia Law Review*, Vol. 33, 1933, pp. 55–56, p. 56.

[70] Jerome Hall, *General Principles of Criminal Law*, Indianapolis, Ind.: Bobbs-Merrill Company, 1947, pp. 304–305.

The Court again addressed the importance of criminal intent in 1952 in *Morissette v. United States*.[71] This case is important because Justice Robert H. Jackson identified limits on the growing trend toward criminal penalties in the absence of a requirement proving criminal intent. He first reviewed the history of what he called "public welfare offenses," which resulted from the increasing complexity of life after the industrial revolution:

> The crimes there involved depend on no mental element but consist only of forbidden acts or omissions. This, while not expressed by the Court, is made clear from examination of a century-old but accelerating tendency, discernible both here and in England, to call into existence new duties and crimes which disregard any ingredient of intent.[72]

In Jackson's view, this was justified by the increasing complexity of contemporary life:

> The industrial revolution multiplied the number of workmen exposed to injury from increasingly powerful and complex mechanisms, driven by freshly discovered sources of energy, requiring higher precautions by employers. Traffic of velocities, volumes and varieties unheard of came to subject the wayfarer to intolerable casualty risks if owners and drivers were not to observe new cares and uniformities of conduct. Congestion of cities and crowding of quarters called for health and welfare regulations undreamed of in simpler times. Wide distribution of goods became an instrument of wide distribution of harm when those who dispersed food, drink, drugs, and even securities, did not comply with reasonable standards of quality, integrity, disclosure and care. Such dangers have engendered increasingly numerous and detailed regulations which heighten the duties of those in control of particular industries, trades, properties or activities that affect public health, safety or welfare.[73]

---

[71] 342 U.S. 246 (1952).

[72] *Morissette*, 342 U.S. at 252–253.

[73] *Morissette*, 342 U.S. at 252–253.

Jackson distinguished conventional criminal offenses, for which specific intent is presumed, from public-welfare offenses, for which it is not:

> Many of these offenses are not in the nature of positive aggressions or invasions, with which the common law so often dealt, but are in the nature of neglect where the law requires care, or inaction where it imposes a duty.[74]

Jackson also sketched a distinction between regulatory offenses and more-serious crimes:

> Stealing, larceny, and its variants and equivalents, were among the earliest offenses known to the law that existed before legislation; they are invasions of rights of property which stir a sense of insecurity in the whole community and arouse public demand for retribution, the penalty is high and, when a sufficient amount is involved, the infamy is that of a felony, which, says Maitland, is . . . as bad a word as you can give to man or thing.[75]

Jackson suggests that the public opprobrium that attaches to a crime—what others have called the blaming function[76]—is relevant to whether criminal intent should be ignored. The Court therefore held that, because the crime of which Morissette was accused was essentially theft, a finding of intent was required for conviction—despite the fact that such a finding was not mentioned as an element in the statute.

*Morissette* is important both because it lays out a pragmatic justification for the growth in criminal statutes that ignore criminal intent and because it identifies a logical limit to this trend.

In the 1950s, the American Law Institute developed the MPC as an authoritative guide for state and federal criminal codes. Its authors

---

[74] *Morissette*, 342 U.S. at 254–256.

[75] *Morissette*, 342 U.S. at 260–261 (citing Frederick Pollock and Frederic William Maitland, *The History of English Law Before the Time of Edward I*, 2nd ed., London: Cambridge University Press, 1968, p. 465).

[76] See Buell, 2006.

announced a "frontal attack" on strict criminal liability for serious offenses.[77] Building on Jackson's distinction, the MPC also adopted a division between "public welfare offenses," which did not require *mens rea*, and traditional crimes. In fact, the MPC required *mens rea* as an element of any offense except those that involve comparatively minimal sanctions and no possibility of imprisonment.[78] Similarly, a large academic literature developed criticizing strict-liability criminal offenses.[79]

The 1970s occasioned an increased focus on corporate crime and an accompanying concern that historical principles of criminal liability were being ignored. The Sherman Antitrust Act, which prohibits antitrust activity, was amended to increase its penalties and make violations felonies.[80] A raft of new regulatory statutes contained criminal penalties without any requirement of criminal intent.[81]

---

[77] MPC § 2.05, comment (American Law Institute, 1955).

[78] MPC §§ 1.04(5), 2.05(1)(a) (American Law Institute, 1962).

[79] See, e.g., Gerhard O. W. Mueller, "On Common Law Mens Rea," *Minnesota Law Review*, Vol. 42, No. 6, May 1958, pp. 1043–1104 (arguing against strict-liability offenses); Anthony A. Cuomo, "*Mens Rea* and Status Criminality," *Southern California Law Review*, Vol. 40, No. 3, Spring 1967, pp. 463–528; and James J. Hippard, Sr., "The Unconstitutionality of Criminal Liability Without Fault: An Argument for a Constitutional Doctrine of Mens Rea," *Houston Law Review*, Vol. 10, No. 5, July 1973, pp. 1039–1058.

[80] See, e.g., U.S. Code, Title 15, Commerce and Trade, Chapter 1, Monopolies and Combinations in Restraint of Trade, Section 1, Trusts, etc., in Restraint of Trade Illegal—Penalty, 1976; U.S. Code, Title 15, Commerce and Trade, Chapter 1, Monopolies and Combinations in Restraint of Trade, Section 2, Monopolizing Trade a Felony—Penalty, 1976; U.S. Code, Title 15, Commerce and Trade, Chapter 1, Monopolies and Combinations in Restraint of Trade, Section 3, Trusts in Territories or District of Columbia Illegal—Combination a Felony, 1976 (the three sections together reclassifying violations of § 1 of the Sherman Antitrust Act from misdemeanor to felony, increasing maximum fines for individuals from $50,000 to $100,000, and increasing maximum term of imprisonment from one year to three years; also creating corporate fines of up to $1 million).

[81] See, e.g., U.S. Code, Title 7, Agriculture, Chapter 21, Tobacco Statistics, Section 503, Reports—Necessity, by Whom Made, Penalties, 1976; U.S. Code, Title 7, Agriculture, Chapter 20, Dumping or Destruction of Interstate Produce, Section 491, Destruction or Dumping of Farm Produce Received in Interstate Commerce by Commission Merchants, etc.—Penalty, 1976; 12 U.S.C. § 378 (1976); U.S. Code, Title 15, Commerce and Trade, Chapter 2A, Securities and Trust Indentures, Subchapter III, Trust Indentures, Section 77yyy, Penalties, 1976; U.S. Code, Title 15, Commerce and Trade, Chapter 2B, Securities Exchanges, Section 78dd-1, Prohibited Foreign Trade Practices by Issuers, 1976; U.S.

These new laws were accompanied by a renewed focus on criminal prosecutions by DOJ.[82] In *United States v. Park*,[83] the U.S. Supreme Court reaffirmed its holding in *Dotterweich* that a corporate officer could be held criminally liable absent any intent. These developments renewed concern about the expanding scope of criminal liability.[84]

In the wake of these developments, in 1978, in *United States v. United States Gypsum Co.*,[85] the Court addressed the question of whether intent was required for criminal liability under the Sherman Antitrust Act, absent a requirement in the statute. The Court, citing

---

Code, Title 15, Commerce and Trade, Chapter 2B, Securities Exchanges, Section 78dd-2, Prohibited Foreign Trade Practices by Domestic Concerns, 1976; U.S. Code, Title 15, Commerce and Trade, Chapter 2B, Securities Exchanges, Section 78ff, Penalties, 1976; U.S. Code, Title 15, Commerce and Trade, Chapter 2, Federal Trade Commission—Promotion of Export Trade and Prevention of Unfair Methods of Competition, Subchapter I, Federal Trade Commission, Section 50, Offenses and Penalties, 1976; U.S. Code, Title 15, Commerce and Trade, Chapter 2, Federal Trade Commission—Promotion of Export Trade and Prevention of Unfair Methods of Competition, Subchapter I, Federal Trade Commission, Section 54, False Advertisements—Penalties, 1976; U.S. Code, Title 15, Commerce and Trade, Chapter 16A, Emergency Petroleum Allocation, Section 754, Omitted, 1976; U.S. Code, Title 15, Commerce and Trade, Chapter 53, Toxic Substances Control, Subchapter I, Control of Toxic Substances, Section 2614, Prohibited Acts, 1976; U.S. Code, Title 15, Commerce and Trade, Chapter 53, Toxic Substances Control, Subchapter I, Control of Toxic Substances, Section 2615, Penalties, 1976; U.S. Code, Title 21, Food and Drugs, Chapter 12, Meat Inspection, Subchapter IV, Auxiliary Provisions, Section 676, Violations, 1976; U.S. Code, Title 33, Navigation and Navigable Waters, Chapter 26, Water Pollution Prevention and Control, Subchapter III, Standards and Enforcement, Section 1319, Enforcement, 1976.

82 See, e.g., "Saxbe to Get Tough with Price-Fixers," *Antitrust and Trade Regulation Report*, No. 683, October 8, 1974, p. A-5 (Attorney General Saxbe described the following DOJ policy: "The emphasis on criminal anti-trust cases will continue—particularly on price fixing. . . . [W]e will generally seek prison terms—for all who are convicted or who plead guilty or no contest. The time for unequal justice is long since past").

83 421 U.S. 658 (1975).

84 See, e.g., Abrams, 1981, pp. 476–477 (criticizing strict liability), p. 475 (arguing that "we tend to resist the idea of strict criminal liability, and our resistance often takes the form of reinterpreting the applicable doctrine to introduce a limited measure of culpability"); see also Kathleen F. Brickey, "Criminal Liability of Corporate Officers for Strict Liability Offenses—Another View," *Vanderbilt Law Review*, Vol. 35, No. 6, November 1982b, pp. 1337–1382 (responding to Abrams).

85 438 U.S. 422 (1978).

and quoting Jackson's opinion in *Morissette*, held that proof of criminal intent was required.[86]

More recently, in 1994, the Supreme Court addressed the role of criminal intent in *Staples v. United States*.[87] In that case, the issue in question was whether a federal statute that criminalized the ownership of a fully automatic weapon—a machine gun—required the government to prove that the defendant knew that the firearm in question could be operated in a fully automatic fashion. The Court held that, despite the absence of any express intent requirement in the statute, Congress did not intend to eliminate intent from this offense. The Court explained, "the existence of a *mens rea* is the rule of, rather than the exception to, the principles of Anglo-American criminal jurisprudence."[88] In reaching this conclusion, the Court also relied, in part, on the fact that defendants could be imprisoned for up to ten years.

Finally, in 2005, the Court addressed the issue of criminal intent for a corporate defendant in the Arthur Andersen case, which we discuss in the next chapter.

## Conclusion

What lessons do we draw from this brief history? First, there is the familiarity of the debate. Recent arguments about the possible unfairness of applying criminal law without an explicit finding of *mens rea* are not novel. There is a long history of both organizations and their directors being found vicariously liable without criminal intent. There has been almost an equally long history of concern over the practice.[89]

Second, the notion that criminal responsibility in Anglo-American law has always required criminal intent is, at best, riddled with exceptions. Nearly 140 years ago, for example, Holmes influen-

---

86 *United States Gypsum Co.*, 438 U.S. at 436–437.

87 511 U.S. 600 (1994).

88 *Staples*, 511 U.S. at 605.

89 See, e.g., *Morissette*, 342 U.S. at 256 (noting misgivings about dispensing with the traditional requirement of *mens rea*).

tially argued that the primary purpose of criminal law was to deter dangerous activities and not to punish wrongful behavior, necessarily making the defendant's intent less important. And although this debate is far from resolved, it is highly unlikely that a sweeping rule that bans criminal prosecutions absent individual criminal intent will now emerge. Arguing that applications of the criminal law in the corporate context *must* require a showing of criminal intent is inconsistent with this history.

Third, the underlying motivation for the development of both vicarious individual liability and corporate liability was pragmatic. As Professor Kathleen F. Brickey observed, in the early cases, these liabilities served "well-defined objectives." Holmes also emphasized the pragmatic rather than moral justification for criminal liability. And in the midcentury cases, "lawmakers, whether wisely or not" attached criminal penalties to make the laws more effective.[90] Again, the rationale was pragmatism, rather than any fidelity to theoretical justifications of punishment.[91] Organizations were thought more likely to comply with regulations if criminal penalties were attached to their violations.

To put it in terms of theories of justification for punishment, the goal was deterrence rather than retribution. This has important implications for the use of the criminal law in this context. If the goal of the punishment is simply to deter misconduct—rather than punish morally guilty organizations and individuals—the efficacy of that criminal punishment in deterring misconduct can and should be measured and compared with other methods. It may be that criminal sanctions are the most effective means to deter misconduct. But it may also be that civil sanctions are sufficient or even more effective. It is ultimately an empirical question, requiring a substantially different and much more instrumental analysis than that usually conducted when thinking about whether some action that provokes moral outrage (e.g., murder) should be criminalized.

---

[90] Justice Jackson's opinion in *Morissette*, 342 U.S. 246.

[91] See also Brickey, 1982a, p. 422 (emphasizing pragmatic justifications for vicarious criminal liability).

Relatedly, most of the cases in which the criminal law was first applied to corporations or that criminal intent was excused involved fines and crimes other than felonies. The more serious the offense—when "the infamy is that of a felony"—the more hesitant the courts usually are to excuse the requirement that the government prove criminal intent. This was true in both *Morissette* and, more recently, in *Staples* and *Arthur Andersen LLP v. United States.*[92]

Finally, although it is easy to identify exceptions to the general rule that individual criminal intent is required in criminal cases, it remains the general rule. Although the pragmatic justifications for moving away from that model may justify it, an abandonment of criminal intent is still the exception. As such, it may lead to costs in perceived procedural fairness.

CHAPTER THREE

# Recent History: A Shift to Reforming Corporations from Within

In Chapter Two, we reviewed the history of corporate prosecutions and the relaxation of the traditional requirements of proving criminal intent that made this possible. We noted that, "whether wisely or not" (in Justice Jackson's phrase), Congress has passed many laws that included criminal penalties without requiring criminal intent. We now turn to more-recent history and focus on DOJ policies of the past 30 years in some detail. This recent history is important to understand how we came to the recent rise in the use of DPAs and NPAs.

We first describe the pre–Federal Sentencing Guidelines for Organizations regime, which prosecuted corporations with relatively small fines in an era in which compliance programs within corporations were relatively small and underdeveloped. We turn to the Sentencing Reform Act of 1984 and the Federal Sentencing Guidelines for Organizations of 1991, which dramatically increased the importance of compliance programs and emphasized the goal of structurally reforming the corporation. But the restructuring was initially a requirement of probation and therefore occurred only after a corporation was convicted. Over time, the importance of compliance programs and restructuring moved up in the criminal process and became a criterion on which a decision to prosecute was made.

We also describe the downfall of Arthur Andersen in 2002, a pivotal case that carried a powerful message to both corporate directors and prosecutors. For directors, the fate of Andersen highlighted the potentially firm-ending risks of taking a case to trial. For prosecutors, the end of Andersen and its effect on thousands of innocent employees and stakeholders highlighted the potential collateral damage that aggressively pursuing a corporate prosecution can entail.

Perhaps as a result of this renewed appreciation of the downsides of conventional criminal proceedings, DPAs and NPAs became much more popular. These allowed prosecutors to accomplish their objective of reforming the corporation without the risk, expense, and delay of trial, and they permitted corporations to avoid the collateral consequences of formal prosecution.

But the proliferation of these agreements has created its own complications. It partly represents the increasing privatization of a historically public function—prosecuting and enforcing the criminal law. For example, private-sector compliance monitors hired by the companies ensure that the terms of the NPA or DPA are met and can investigate culpable individuals. In addition, corporations also have increased incentives to investigate potential wrongdoing before the government learns of the problem and potentially disclose information inculpating individual defendants to federal prosecutors. But these private actors do not have the same checks and balances that public prosecutors and police face. Although DPA-required monitors may be effective tools to reform errant corporations, their profusion calls for increased scrutiny and an appreciation of their disadvantages.

## The Traditional Approach: Prosecuting the Corporation, Not Individuals

Prior to the 1990s, DOJ focused relatively more on prosecuting corporations than individuals when targeting corporate criminal liability.[1] Between 1988 and 1990, for example, no individual defendant was convicted in one-third of cases in which an organization was also sen-

1 Jennifer Arlen, "Removing Prosecutors from the Boardroom: Limiting Prosecutorial Discretion to Impose Structural Reforms," in Anthony S. Barkow and Rachel E. Barkow, eds., *Prosecutors in the Boardroom: Using Criminal Law to Regulate Corporate Conduct*, New York: New York University Press, 2011, pp. 62–86.

tenced for a crime (except antitrust offenses).[2] Corporate sanctions were also comparatively small and typically involved fines similar in magnitude to ones levied against individuals who were convicted of similar offenses. For example, Cohen found that 60 percent of corporations sentenced in federal court were fined $10,000, and the average was just $45,790.[3] DPAs and other efforts at structural reform of the offending firm were extremely uncommon. Because the fines were relatively modest, the incentive effects of the criminal liability were also comparatively limited.

As a result of this regime, corporations also had limited incentives to actively police themselves or report potentially criminal wrongdoing to authorities. For example, under longstanding Delaware corporate law of the era, directors were not required to adopt a compliance program absent notice of wrongdoing. The opinion in the leading case of the era explained that "there is no duty upon the directors to install and operate a corporate system of espionage to ferret out wrongdoing which they have no reason to suspect exists."[4] As a result, firms had limited incentives to develop compliance programs. Indeed, as commentators have pointed out, firms had incentives *not* to develop compliance programs or to discover wrongdoing because any such discovery could, in fact, lead to civil or criminal liability that might not otherwise exist. Thus, there were considerable incentives for corporate directors to adopt a head-in-the-sand approach with respect to potential criminal activity.

The absence of robust corporate compliance programs meant that that individual offenders were less likely to be caught. Unlike many other crimes, crime that takes place within an organization is often difficult to detect. Even once criminal activity is suspected or detected, it can be very difficult for outside agencies to identify the culpable parties. Developing a case beyond a reasonable doubt against a particular

---

2 Mark A. Cohen, "Corporate Crime and Punishment: An Update on Sentencing Practice in the Federal Courts, 1988–1990," *Boston University Law Review*, Vol. 71, No. 2, March 1991, pp. 247–280, p. 268.

3 Cohen, 1991, pp. 254–256.

4 *Graham v. Allis-Chalmers Mfg. Co.*, 188 A.2d 125, 130 (Del. 1963).

individual is even more difficult. The complex, decentralized nature of organizations can also mean that the individuals who commit criminal actions may not be the most culpable and may be doing so at the direction or suggestion of someone else.

The focus on prosecuting corporations rather than individuals in this era also differentially affected the incentives facing closely held, as opposed to publicly traded, corporations. As Jennifer Arlen has noted, vicarious corporate criminal liability is arguably more effective at deterring crime in closely held corporations than for large publicly traded companies.[5] In closely held corporations, the owners of the firm are often the managers. By placing the criminal liability on the organization itself, the owner's interest in the firm is directly affected. This creates incentives for the owner/managers to prevent criminal wrongdoing.

In contrast, for large publicly held corporations, the incentives are more diffuse. Unless the perpetrator has a substantial equity position in the firm, criminal sanctions applied to the firm may not directly act as a deterrent. Although the shareholders have an interest in having the firm itself police employees to prevent criminal activity that harms the value of the company, this set of incentives is more indirect than those that exist in the privately held corporation and the familiar principal-agency problems associated with divergent management and shareholder interests can apply. On the other hand, many compensation packages for chief executive officers (CEOs) are tied to share prices, and most directors are likely to want to avoid criminal investigations, so this distinction between the incentives facing directors of privately held and public corporations may be more theoretical than actual.

[5] Arlen, 2011, pp. 69–70.

## Guidelines Era: The Start of Structural Reforms

In 1984, the Sentencing Reform Act[6] accomplished a vast change in federal sentencing for both the individual and the corporation. The law was enacted by an unusual coalition of liberals and conservatives.[7] Liberals expressed concern that judicial discretion was undermining the rule of law because some defendants received unequal sentences. Conservatives were generally concerned with what they perceived as undue leniency in sentencing. The result was a regime that permitted individual judges far less individual discretion and generally increased sentences and fines.[8] In the context of corporate law, this dynamic was manifested by the enactment of the Federal Sentencing Guidelines for Organizations from 1991 that put a new emphasis on (1) imposing structural changes on convicted organizations, (2) increasing fines, (3) prosecuting individuals, and (4) prosecuting a corporation only if it neglected compliance.

### Imposing Structural Changes

The guidelines increased the role of structural changes in response to corporate crimes. The introductory comment to the Federal Sentencing Guidelines for Organizations emphasized the need to undertake systemic changes at the organization:

> [P]robation is an appropriate sentence for an organizational defendant when needed to ensure that another sanction will be fully implemented, or to ensure that steps will be taken within the organization to reduce the likelihood of future criminal conduct.

---

6 U.S. Code, Title 28, Judiciary and Judicial Procedure, Part III, Court Officers and Employees, Chapter 58, United States Sentencing Commission, Section 991, United States Sentencing Commission—Establishment and Purposes, 1988.

7 See generally Kate Stith and José A. Cabranes, *Fear of Judging: Sentencing Guidelines in the Federal Courts*, Chicago, Ill.: University of Chicago Press, 1998, pp. 38–48.

8 James M. Anderson, Jeffrey R. Kling, and Kate Stith, "Measuring Interjudge Sentencing Disparity: Before and After the Federal Sentencing Guidelines," *Journal of Law and Economics*, Vol. 42, No. S1, April 1999, pp. 271–308.

> These guidelines offer incentives to organizations to reduce and ultimately eliminate criminal conduct by providing a structural foundation from which an organization may self-police its own conduct through an effective compliance and ethics program. The prevention and detection of criminal conduct, as facilitated by an effective compliance and ethics program, will assist an organization in encouraging ethical conduct and in complying fully with all applicable laws.[9]

The guidelines expanded the circumstances under which a judge was required to impose probation on a corporation.[10] It also increased the range of structural changes that prosecutors could enact as part of probation. These include the condition that the organization not commit another federal, state, or local crime; restitution; community service; and "other conditions that . . . are reasonably related to the nature and circumstances of the offense."[11] The guidelines also emphasized the development of compliance and ethics programs as a condition of probation.[12]

Probation substantially raised the effective penalty on a corporation for a subsequent violation because the corporation could be punished for the violation of the terms of probation in addition to whatever penalties accompanied the new offense.

### Increasing Fines

Prior to the 1980s, corporations were generally punished by using the same sanctions that were set out in the statute as applicable to individual defendants. The deterrent effect, however, of a $10,000 fine is likely to be substantially greater for an individual defendant than for a large or even midsized corporation that grosses millions of dollars annually.

---

[9] U.S. Sentencing Commission, *Federal Sentencing Guidelines Manual*, Washington, D.C., 2011, p. 504.

[10] U.S. Sentencing Commission, 2011, § 8D1.1(a) (enumerating circumstances under which "the court shall order a term of probation").

[11] U.S. Sentencing Commission, 2011, § 8D1.3(c).

[12] U.S. Sentencing Commission, 2011, § 8D1.4(b)(1).

Beginning in the 1980s, Congress increased the sanctions applicable to corporations and directed the U.S. Sentencing Commission to set forth sentencing guidelines applicable to organizations separately from those applicable to individuals. In response, in 1991, the U.S. Sentencing Commission enacted the Federal Sentencing Guidelines for Organizations. These substantially increased the fines that corporations paid and also included nonfine sanctions, including restitution to victims of the criminal offense and remediation, where possible.[13]

Empirical research indicates that these efforts successfully increased the criminal fines paid by defendant organizations. After publication of the guidelines, criminal fines imposed on publicly held corporations increased an order of magnitude, from $1.9 million to $19 million (in 1996 dollars).[14] In cases governed by the Federal Sentencing Guidelines for Organizations, median fines went from $633,000 to $3.1 million.[15] In an effort to measure the guidelines' effect on total sanctions, one study summed criminal fines, nonfine criminal monetary sanctions, government civil penalties, and private civil sanctions. The study found that these sanctions, on average, for convicted publicly held companies went from $13.3 million before the guidelines to more than $49 million afterward.[16]

### Prosecuting Individual Defendants

The Sentencing Reform Act that created the guidelines was also motivated, in part, by concern that white-collar defendants were receiving overly lenient sentences and that judges were reluctant to send white-collar offenders to prison.[17] Prior to publication of the guidelines,

---

13 U.S. Sentencing Commission, 2011, §§ 8B1 ("Remedying Harm from Criminal Conduct"), 8D1.1 ("Imposition of Probation: Organizations").

14 C. Alexander, Arlen, and Cohen, 1999, p. 410.

15 C. Alexander, Arlen, and Cohen, 1999.

16 C. Alexander, Arlen, and Cohen, 1999, p. 420.

17 See U.S. Senate, *P.L. 98-473, Continuing Appropriations, 1985—Comprehensive Crime Control Act of 1984*, S. Rep. 98-225, August 4, 1983, p. 177. Liberals who supported the Sentencing Reform Act expressed concern that white-collar criminals were not punished sufficiently. See generally Stith and Cabranes, 1998, pp. 38–48.

white-collar criminals were much less likely to go to prison than non–white-collar criminals who stole similar amounts, and, when they did go to prison, their sentences were substantially shorter.[18]

Consistently with this legislative sentiment, DOJ focused more on prosecuting individuals than the corporation.[19] Similarly, the typical sentences sought by prosecutors increased in severity, with a shift from probation to prison time as the primary component of the sentence.[20] After publication of the guidelines, white-collar sentences of all types increased. Only 30 percent of fraud defendants were sentenced to just probation, in comparison with the 57 percent who received that sentence before there were guidelines.[21] In addition, the Sentencing Commission twice raised the individual guideline sentences for theft and fraud of all types, in 1998 and 2001.[22]

### Emphasizing Compliance Programs

Not only were compliance programs routinely incorporated in conditions of probation but they were also employed as a way of reducing liability after conviction. The Federal Sentencing Guidelines for Organizations mandated lower fines for corporations with effective

---

[18] Stephen Breyer, "The Federal Sentencing Guidelines and the Key Compromises Upon Which They Rest," *Hofstra Law Review*, Vol. 17, No. 1, Fall 1988, pp. 1–50, p. 20. Statistics collected by the Sentencing Commission showed that, before the guidelines existed, 57 percent of fraud defendants received probation (U.S. Sentencing Commission, *Supplementary Report on the Initial Sentencing Guidelines and Policy Statements*, June 18, 1987, pp. 68–69, Tables 2 and 3).

[19] Arlen, 2011, p. 74.

[20] Arlen, 2011.

[21] Frank O. Bowman III, "A Challenge to the Rationale for General Economic Crime Sentence Increases Following Sarbanes-Oxley: Letter of Frank Bowman to U.S. Sentencing Commission," *Federal Sentencing Reporter*, Vol. 15, No. 4, April 2003a, pp. 284–290, pp. 286–287, Figures 5a and 5c.

[22] U.S. Sentencing Commission, "Sentencing Guidelines for United States Courts," *Federal Register*, Vol. 66, No. 109, June 6, 2001, pp. 30512–30563, p. 30,540 (stating the Sentencing Commission's reasons for consolidating guidelines for theft and fraud); U.S. Sentencing Commission, "Sentencing Guidelines for United States Courts," *Federal Register*, Vol. 63, No. 229, November 30, 1998, pp. 65979–65993, pp. 65,982–65,992.

compliance programs.[23] Similarly, the guidelines called for a less severe penalty for any firm that reported the misconduct promptly upon its discovery and cooperated fully with federal authorities.[24]

Although the guidelines encouraged the development of compliance programs and cooperation with the government in enforcement, some felt that the guidelines did not go far enough in reducing penalties for firms with compliance programs. Arlen, for example, argued that criminal liability still resulted in "enormous negative consequences . . . as a result of collateral penalties, civil damages actions, and in some situations, enhanced reputational penalties."[25]

Although this incentive regime was an improvement over the incentives for director ignorance created by the approach in place before the guidelines existed, the enormous consequences of a criminal conviction might still deter the development of a robust program to discover problems. For the rational firm, the disadvantages of discovering criminal activity and the subsequent conviction might outweigh the postconviction advantages of having a robust compliance program.

In the early years of the guidelines, a preference emerged for restructuring corporations found guilty of crimes. Through outside monitors, corporate probation, and the importance of cooperation for Federal Sentencing Guidelines calculation after an offense is identified and prosecuted, prosecutors and the Sentencing Commission emphasized the goal of improving and restructuring the errant organization

---

[23] U.S. Sentencing Commission, 2011, § 8C2.5(f) ("Effective Compliance and Ethics Program").

[24] U.S. Sentencing Commission, 2011, § 8C2.5(g)(1):

> If the organization (A) prior to an imminent threat of disclosure or government investigation; and (B) within a reasonably prompt time after becoming aware of the offense, reported the offense to appropriate governmental authorities, fully cooperated in the investigation, and clearly demonstrated recognition and affirmative acceptance of responsibility for its criminal conduct, subtract 5 points.

[25] Arlen, 2011, p. 75. Among the most serious of the collateral consequences was debarment—being banned from doing business with the federal government. This "collateral" penalty could have the effect of essentially ending companies for which the federal government is a major customer. Similarly, federal or state regulators could be required to revoke licenses that are necessary for the firms' core businesses. As we explain in the next chapter, debarment actions have increased substantially in the past several years.

rather than punishing it. It accomplished this by requiring firms to create compliance programs to ensure that the problems that led to federal investigation were eliminated. It is striking how similar this goal was to one of the classical goals of criminal law—rehabilitation of the offender.[26]

## The Rise of the Nonprosecution Agreement

Beginning in the late 1990s, prosecutors more aggressively sought to reform the corporation itself by using DPAs and NPAs. In this section, we discuss the policy changes that DOJ made for corporate prosecutions. These new directions in policy both help explain some of the variation that we observe in corporate prosecutions and, at times, prove controversial as a matter of procedural law.

### Holder Memorandum

The first steps toward the increasing role of compliance and cooperation occurred in the late 1990s. To centralize guidance for federal prosecutors, Deputy Attorney General Eric Holder issued a policy statement in 1999 titled "Bringing Criminal Charges Against Corporations" (the "Holder memorandum").[27] Although the memorandum encouraged prosecution of culpable corporations, it also emphasized compliance and cooperation as key criteria for prosecutors to use in deciding whether to prosecute a corporation. Rather than simply reducing the penalties sought by DOJ in exchange for alternative approaches, the Holder memorandum stated that prosecutors should not prosecute

[26] This is all the more remarkable because this development occurred at perhaps the nadir of the importance placed on rehabilitation in U.S. criminal law. Individualized rehabilitation of offenders as a goal or justification of punishment was deemphasized and sometimes thought naïve in the 1980s and early 1990s, with numerous jurisdictions abandoning indeterminate sentencing for individuals and retribution, deterrence, and incapacitation being touted as the central goals of criminal law. Yet in this very same period, prosecutors worked at reforming organizations rather than individuals.

[27] Eric Holder, deputy attorney general, "Bringing Criminal Charges Against Corporations," memorandum to all component heads and U.S. Attorneys, Washington, D.C., June 16, 1999.

firms that met their enforcement duties. The possibility of getting a corporation to voluntarily agree to a having compliance program became a key aspect of any DOJ decision whether to prosecute an organization, not just something to incorporate into a sentence after conviction. However, the memorandum still left considerable discretion with individual prosecutors.

### Thompson Memorandum: Use of Aggressive Litigation Strategies to Change Corporations

In 2001, Enron collapsed as a result of major accounting fraud. WorldCom followed shortly thereafter. There was considerable political pressure to address white-collar crime.[28] On July 30, 2002, President George W. Bush signed SOX, which substantially increased the penalties for fraudulent financial activity. In January 2003, a memorandum issued by then–Deputy Attorney General Larry Thompson superseded the Holder memorandum.[29]

The Thompson memorandum took a relatively aggressive and encompassing view of corporate criminal liability but also suggested "pretrial diversion" as an important tool for prosecutors seeking to "alter corporate behavior." DPAs and NPAs became key components for pretrial diversion programs, as well as an effective way to reform corporations from within.

Although neither the potentially expansive scope of corporate liability based on the actions of employees of the organization nor the use of pretrial diversion and NPAs or DPAs was entirely new, the Thompson memorandum resulted in more-aggressive use of NPAs and DPAs in subsequent years.

The Thompson memorandum also suggested the use of several potent but controversial new litigation strategies in the quest to reform wayward corporations. These included discouraging corporations from

---

28 See generally Frank O. Bowman III, "Editor's Observations: The Sarbanes-Oxley Act and What Came After," *Federal Sentencing Reporter*, Vol. 15, No. 4, April 2003b, pp. 231–233, p. 231.

29 Larry D. Thompson, deputy attorney general, "Principles of Federal Prosecution of Business Organizations," memorandum to heads of department components and U.S. Attorneys, January 20, 2003.

providing counsel to individual defendants and encouraging corporations to waive the attorney–client privilege in order to qualify as having cooperating with the government for purposes of either avoiding formal charges or seeking leniency at sentencing. The memorandum suggested, "too often business organizations, while purporting to cooperate with a Department investigation, in fact take steps to impede the quick and effective exposure of the complete scope of wrongdoing under investigation." The Thompson memorandum similarly suggested that the use of joint defense agreements would be seen as evidence that the corporation was not sincere in its desire to cooperate with the government.[30]

Although these litigation strategies may have aided DOJ in investigating corporate misfeasance, they encountered considerable opposition from many academic commentators, the corporate bar, and, on occasion, the federal bench. The Thompson memorandum signified the high-water mark of the use of aggressive litigation strategies to change corporations. As we discuss, DOJ subsequently reduced its use of these aggressive tactics.

Ironically, these measures may have also undermined DOJ's stated goal of reforming the corporation from within by strengthening compliance programs. By potentially requiring the general counsel to reveal communications with employees, these efforts created disincentives for an employee to report possible misconduct or issues of questionable legality to a company's lawyers, potentially inadvertently hindering efforts at improving governance.

### The Fall of Arthur Andersen

The downfall of the professional services firm Arthur Andersen in 2002 may have accelerated the use of DPAs and NPAs and continues to serve as a touchstone in the debates over the appropriate level of criminal intent in corporate prosecutions.

In September 2001, Enron was having serious difficulties. Its CEO, Jeffrey Skilling, abruptly resigned on August 14, and Michael C.

[30] A joint defense agreement allows information to be shared between two parties (e.g., a defendant corporation and an individual defendant) while still protecting the attorney–client privilege in that information.

Odom, a partner at Arthur Andersen partly responsible for Enron, was warned of looming problems with Enron's accounting. Andersen anticipated litigation and, on October 8, retained outside counsel to represent it. On October 10, Odom spoke at a training meeting that included ten individuals who worked on the Enron team. At this training, he urged everyone to comply with the firm's document-retention policy. According to the Supreme Court, he said,

> [I]f it's destroyed in the course of [the] normal policy and litigation is filed the next day, that's great. . . . [W]e've followed our own policy, and whatever there was that might have been of interest to somebody is gone and irretrievable.[31]

Andersen's document-retention policy called for a single engagement file that "should contain only that information which is relevant to supporting our work."[32] The policy also stated that, "in cases of threatened litigation, . . . . No related information will be destroyed." In a separate provision, the policy noted that, if Andersen is advised of litigation or subpoenas regarding a particular engagement, the related information should not be destroyed.

On October 19, Enron forwarded a letter indicating that the SEC had launched an investigation into Andersen. On October 20, the Enron crisis-response team within Andersen held a conference call. Nancy A. Temple, a lawyer employed by Enron, instructed everyone to make sure that they followed the document-retention policy. On October 23, David B. Duncan, the head of the Andersen–Enron engagement team, told the other partners at Andersen on the Enron team to ensure that their team members were complying with the document-retention policy. On October 30, the SEC opened a formal investigation and requested accounting documents. On November 8, the SEC served Enron and Andersen with subpoenas for records. Throughout

---

[31] *United States v. Andersen*, 374 F. 3d 281, 286 (5th Cir. 2004).

[32] *Arthur Andersen LLP v. United States*, 544 U.S. at n. 4.

this period, considerable paper and electronic document destruction occurred.[33]

After investigation of this chronology, Andersen was offered a plea deal to permit it to avoid indictment if it publicly acknowledged that it illegally destroyed documents and agreed to restrictions that were similar to probation.[34] This would have been one of the first large-scale DPAs.[35] However, apparently Andersen officials felt that such an admission would be just as destructive as an indictment or guilty plea, and they believed that they had broken no law.[36] Instead, they decided to take the case to trial.

In March 2002, Andersen was indicted in the Southern District of Texas on one count of violating 18 U.S.C. §§ 1512(b)(2)(A) and (B). The specific allegation was that, between October 10 and November 9, Andersen "did knowingly, intentionally and corruptly persuade . . . other persons, to wit: Andersen's employees, with intent to cause" them to withhold documents from and alter documents for use in "official proceedings."

At trial, a critical issue was the issue of criminal intent. The government's theory was that Andersen violated the federal law that made it a crime to "knowingly . . . corruptly persuade another person . . . with intent to cause" that person to "withhold" or "alter" documents in an "official proceeding."[37] Despite this statutory language, the jury instructions that the government sought and that the judge gave did not require the government to prove that individual actors within the firm understood that their actions were illegal, however. The instruc-

---

[33] *Arthur Andersen LLP v. United States*, 544 U.S. at n. 4.

[34] Kurt Eichenwald, "Andersen Refused a Probation Deal," *New York Times*, April 2, 2002.

[35] Eichenwald, 2002.

[36] Eichenwald, 2002. Once Andersen refused this agreement, prosecutors may have felt that they had no choice but to take the case to trial, if only to protect their credibility in negotiations with other companies.

[37] U.S. Code, Title 18, Crimes and Criminal Procedure, Part I, Crimes, Chapter 73, Obstruction of Justice, Section 1512, Tampering with a Witness, Victim, or an Informant, 1976, ¶¶ (b)(2)(A) (withholding testimony, records, documents, or other objects) and (B) (altering, destroying, mutilating, or concealing something with intent to impair its integrity or availability).

tions permitted the jury to convict if they found that Andersen's actions "subvert[ed], undermine[d] or impede[d]" the government's investigation.[38]

On June 15, 2002, Arthur Andersen LLP was convicted for these actions. On August 31, 2002, the firm surrendered its certified public accountant (CPA) license and effectively ceased operations. The disproportionate effect that the actions of a handful of people had on a major organization was striking. Although the indictment alleged the misconduct of only a few individuals, approximately 28,000 employees of Arthur Andersen lost their jobs, the vast majority of whom had no role in or knowledge of the wrongdoing.[39] Retired Andersen partners were also harmed.

The remnant of Andersen appealed the conviction on a variety of grounds, including the jury instruction. On May 31, 2005, the Supreme Court overturned the conviction of Arthur Andersen as a result of flaws in the jury instruction that removed a vital element of *mens rea*, whether the defendant realized that the document destruction was wrongful. The Court noted that it was not illegal to persuade a person to withhold documents from the government and that document-retention policies were appropriately and legally designed to do precisely that.[40] The Court was sharply critical of the jury instructions, noting that jurors were not required to find that the defendants possessed "the requisite consciousness of wrongdoing. Indeed it is striking how little culpability the instructions required."[41] But by this point, Andersen essentially no longer existed.

It seems unlikely that DOJ deliberately set out to destroy Andersen and undertake a prosecution that substantially punished thousands of innocent employees. How did such a thing occur? As is often the case

---

[38] *Arthur Andersen LLP v. United States*, 544 U.S. 696 (2005).

[39] Delroy Alexander, Greg Burns, Robert Manor, Flynn McRoberts, and E. A. Torriero, "The Fall of Andersen," *Hartford Courant*, November 1, 2002; see also Unmesh Kher, "The End of Arthur Andersen?" *Time*, March 11, 2002 (noting that "some of Andersen's most prestigious and loyal clients . . . are cancelling contracts").

[40] *Arthur Andersen LLP v. United States*, 544 U.S. 696 (2005).

[41] *Arthur Andersen LLP v. United States*, 544 U.S. 696 (2005).

in high-profile prosecutions, there was substantial political pressure to find and punish miscreants in the wake of the Enron debacle. And the discovery that Andersen employees were engaged in deliberate destruction of thousands of documents that were germane to the government's investigation surely aroused the ire of DOJ, the SEC, and the public at large.[42] The more populist retributivist urge to punish moral wrongdoing (as opposed to deter future violations) may have had an impact.[43]

The dynamics of plea-bargaining may also have played a role. Even if prosecutors did not want to actually convict the organization, their primary bargaining chip was the threat to indict the company.[44] Once the company turned down the offer of probation, it would have been very difficult politically to back down from the earlier threat to indict. Such a concession in a high- profile case would probably be perceived to undermine DOJ's general credibility in negotiating plea bargains.

---

[42] Mark Tran, "Congress to Investigate Mass Enron Paper Shred," *Guardian*, January 21, 2002.

[43] Alschuler has argued that the instinct to punish a corporation is akin to the medieval practice of deodand, the punishment of inanimate objects associated with a crime:

> We resent crime, and in our rush to express our indignation, we may truly personify and hate the corporation. We may hate the mahogany paneling, the Lear jet, the smokestack, the glass tower, and *all* of the people inside. They—the mahogany and all of them—are responsible for the oil spill, the price-fixing, and the illegal campaign contributions. To superstitious people, villains need not breath; they may include Exxon and the phone company. The corporation thus becomes for some of us, not Frankpledge, but deodand. Just as primitive people hated and punished the wheel of a cart that had run someone over, or the horse that had thrown its rider, or the sword that a murderer had used, some of us truly manage to hate the corporate entity. (Albert Alschuler, "Ancient Law and the Punishment of Corporations: Of Frankpledge and Deodand," *Boston University Law Review*, Vol. 71, 1991, pp. 307–313, p. 312)

[44] Several studies suggest that indictments will harm the value of a firm. For example, Skantz et al. found that when an indictment is announced against a firm for price-fixing, the firm experienced negative abnormal returns (Terrance R. Skantz, Dale O. Cloniger, and Thomas H. Strickland, "Price-Fixing and Shareholder Returns: An Empirical Study," *Financial Review*, Vol. 25, No. 1, February 1990, pp. 153–163, pp. 157–160). Reichert et al. also found that firms experience negative abnormal returns after an indictment, bolstering Skantz, Cloniger, and Strickland's previous findings (Alan K. Reichert, Michael Lockett, and Ramesh P. Rao, "The Impact of Illegal Business Practice on Shareholder Returns," *Financial Review*, Vol. 31, No. 1, February 1996, pp. 67–85, pp. 72–75).

Corporate directors also surely drew lessons from the Andersen prosecution, which highlighted the potential extreme risks of going to trial. Even with what may have appeared to the directors to be a strong defense to this charge (the lack of any proof of criminal intent and the existing document-retention policy), the decision to go to trial led to the destruction of the firm.

### The McNulty and Filip Memoranda

Subsequent to the Supreme Court's decision in *Arthur Andersen LLP v. United States*, DOJ backed away from the more-aggressive positions it had taken in the Thompson memorandum. A policy statement issued in 2006 by Deputy Attorney General Paul J. McNulty moderated several important positions.[45] More recently, guidance about the criminal pursuit of corporations was encompassed in a subsequent policy statement authored by then–Deputy Attorney General Mark R. Filip in 2008, which has expressed a more cautious attitude about corporate prosecutions and a repudiation of some of the more-aggressive litigation tactics of the Thompson memorandum.[46]

More specifically, the Filip memorandum generally disclaimed asking corporate targets not to pay the defense costs of individual defendants. It also stated that prosecutors should generally not consider this factor in deciding whether a corporation is cooperating.[47] It also affirmatively stated that it was not DOJ policy to encourage

---

[45] Paul J. McNulty, deputy attorney general, "Principles of Federal Prosecution of Business Organizations," memorandum to heads of department components and U.S. Attorneys, December 2006.

[46] Mark Filip, deputy attorney general, "Principles of Federal Prosecution of Business Organizations," memorandum to heads of department components and U.S. Attorneys, August 28, 2008.

[47] In a case involving KPMG LLP, the United States asked KPMG not to provide financial assistance to individual defendants. This was harshly criticized by Judge Lewis A. Kaplan, who was presiding over the individual defendant's trial and found a violation of due process:

> [The prosecutor's] deliberate interference with the defendants' rights was outrageous and shocking in the constitutional sense because it was fundamentally at odds with two of our most basic constitutional values—the right to counsel and the right to fair criminal proceedings. (*United States v. Stein*, 495 F. Supp. 2d 390 [S.D.N.Y. 2007])

either work-product or attorney–client privilege waivers: "eligibility for cooperation credit is not predicated upon the waiver of attorney-client privilege or work-product protection." Indeed, under the Filip memorandum, prosecutors were no longer permitted to provide credit to a corporation for waiving either of these privileges.

The Filip memorandum also acknowledged the importance of legal counsel to increase compliance:

> The value of promoting a corporation's ability to seek frank and comprehensive legal advice is particularly important in the contemporary global business environment, where corporations often face complex and dynamic legal and regulatory obligations imposed by the federal government and also by states and foreign governments. . . . For these reasons, waiving the attorney-client and work product protections has never been a prerequisite under the department's prosecution guidelines for a corporation to be viewed as cooperative.[48]

The Filip memorandum also seemed to encourage the further use of DPAs and NPAs. In § 9-2200, discussing general principles of corporate liability, the Filip memorandum includes an important new comment:

> In certain instances, it may be appropriate, upon consideration of the factors set forth herein, to resolve a corporate criminal case by means other than indictment. Non-prosecution and deferred prosecution agreements, for example, occupy an important middle ground between declining prosecution and obtaining the conviction of a corporation.[49]

Moreover, the memorandum encourages prosecutors to consider the collateral effects of a prosecution when deciding whether to use an NPA or DPA. In particular, the memorandum states that prosecutors may consider the following:

---

[48] EOUSA, *United States Attorneys' Manual*, Washington, D.C.: U.S. Department of Justice, 1997, § 9-28.710.

[49] Filip, 2008, § 9-2200.

> possibly substantial consequences to a corporation's employees, investors, pensioners, and customers, many of whom may, depending on the size and nature of the corporation and their role in its operations, have played no role in the criminal conduct, have been unaware of it or have been unable to prevent it.[50]

Under those conditions, the Filip memorandum emphasizes that,

> where the collateral consequences of a corporate conviction for innocent third parties may be significant, [it] may be appropriate to consider a non-prosecution or deferred prosecution agreement with conditions designed, among other things, to promote compliance with applicable law and to prevent recidivism.[51]

Despite the substantial change in tone and substance of the Filip memorandum as compared with its predecessors, corporations still face considerable pressure to show that they are cooperating. This may include sharing otherwise-confidential information and seeking to identify and punish culpable individuals. Although prosecutors cannot request attorney notes or memoranda from lawyer interviews of individuals, prosecutors can still request "relevant factual information acquired through those interviews, unless the identical information has otherwise been provided."[52] Although the Filip memorandum abjured some individual tactics, the underlying dynamics and the corporations' enormous incentives to be found cooperating and thereby avoid prosecution remain substantial.

### Explanations for the Rise in Deferred and Nonprosecution Agreements

Post–*Arthur Andersen LLP v. United States*, potential defendants have sought to avoid indictment, and prosecutors may be more willing to avoid indictment. Firms have reached agreements with prosecutors that allow the firms to avoid indictment conditional on adhering to the

---

[50] EOUSA, 1997, § 9-28.1000.

[51] EOUSA, 1997, § 9-28.1000.

[52] EOUSA, 1997, § 9-28.720.

agreement. These are usually called NPAs or DPAs. The terms of these agreements can vary widely in scope.

These agreements have become much more common in the federal system. By one measurement, only 11 were negotiated between 1993 and 2001, while, just in 2006 to 2008, more than 66 agreements were used.[53]

The agreements have considerable advantages for both the investigated corporation and the prosecution. For the corporation, these agreements avoid indictment and the considerable collateral consequences that indictment or conviction entails. Indictment or conviction may also increase the likelihood that shareholders may file a civil suit against a company. Debarment provisions in some federal and state statutes may prevent a company from doing business with governmental entities if it is indicted. This may also lead to enormous pressure on the corporation to avoid indictment.

Richard A. Epstein has decried what he calls the "grand inversion."[54] He argues that the effective penalties to a corporation that accompany indictment are nearly as great as conviction but are not accompanied by the same procedural protections. Because of the growth of the regulatory state, many businesses require various licenses in order to conduct ordinary business. In some cases, licensing boards are required to end the relevant licenses upon indictment, prior to any proof of guilt.[55]

---

53 Peter Spivack and Sujit Raman, "Regulating the 'New Regulators': Current Trends in Deferred Prosecution Agreements," *American Criminal Law Review*, Vol. 45, 2008, pp. 159–167, p. 167. See Mary Jo White, "Corporate Criminal Liability: What Has Gone Wrong?" *37th Annual Institute on Securities Regulation*, Vol. 2, November 2005, pp. 815–828, p. 818 (discussing use of DPAs as early as 1994).

54 Richard A. Epstein, "Contingent Commissions in Insurance: A Legal and Economic Analysis," *Competition Policy International*, Vol. 3, 2007, p. 281.

55 Epstein (2007) cites U.S. Code, Title 15, Commerce and Trade, Chapter 98, Public Company Accounting Reform and Corporate Responsibility, Subchapter I, Public Company Accounting Oversight Board, Section 7215, Investigations and Disciplinary Proceedings, 1976 (allowing for the suspension or forfeiture of a public accounting firm's registration for failure to cooperate with an investigation of the Public Company Accounting Oversight Board).

In addition to whatever formal elimination of licenses might occur, the reputational damage that a company suffers upon indictment is considerable. Firms may rationally wish to avoid doing business with a company under indictment, well before any proof or admission of guilt. As a result, according to Epstein, "Indictment poses a greater threat than conviction, even though it offers a defendant weaker protections than a convicted criminal." As a result, Epstein expressed concern that companies are desperate to avoid indictment and willing to accept onerous terms; "indeed, sometimes they include concessions that could *never* be obtained through conviction."[56]

From a descriptive perspective, it is clear that, after the fall of Arthur Andersen, there has been a striking rise in DPAs and NPAs. Both companies and prosecutors seem to believe that these agreements are preferable to conventional criminal prosecution. Many of the criticisms leveled against resolving criminal cases with plea agreements are even more applicable to these arrangements.

DPAs and NPAs are attractive to the prosecution because the prosecutor has limited interest in sparking collateral consequences over which he or she has no control. Unleashing hard-to-predict reputational and other collateral consequences that may or may not match the prosecutor's estimates can be problematic, with the *Arthur Andersen LLP v. United States* prosecution being an excellent example.

Perhaps most importantly, DPAs and NPAs further the prosecutor's ability to reform the organization from within. By employing outside monitors and mandating extensive compliance programs, the prosecutor can, at least in theory, change the corporation's internal culture. A key justification for vicarious corporate liability is creating incentives for the corporation to root out criminal activity itself. Proponents have argued that, because of the complexity of corporations and their rational interest in protecting employees, it would be too difficult for outside prosecutors to identify and prosecute individual defendants without vicarious corporate liability to motivate the corporation itself to self-police. DPAs and NPAs are simply another tool for accomplish-

---

[56] Epstein, 2007, p. 41.

ing such self-policing and are arguably superior to a conventional criminal prosecution.

But because DPAs and NPAs are typically negotiated and executed prior to the indictment, there is no judicial oversight over the terms of such agreements, so prosecutors do not have to worry about the risk of a judge rejecting a plea agreement or the terms of probation. In theory, this would allow the prosecutor and the corporation to craft creative, outside-the-box agreements to join forces to minimize the chance of future criminal activity within the corporation. Another advantage of these agreements is that they do not require judicial resources or the considerable costs and delay of a trial. By settling the conflicts early, they reduce the costs on the public fisc.

Finally, there is an increasing recognition in a number of fields that a systems approach to reducing human error is more effective than trying to blame and punish individual miscreants.[57] Crimes that aid the corporation may be more common in organizations that have particular corporate cultures. Reducing these individual offenses may require cultural change within organizations. In this respect, the attempt to accomplish structural change within organizations may be ahead of its time, and DPAs and NPAs might be valuable tools in accomplishing these changes.

However, they also have important disadvantages. First, the scope of these agreements can be vast and far exceed the regulatory power present in most plea bargains. For example, New York State Attorney General Eliot Spitzer sought to change "the way Wall Street operates." After discovering conflicts of interest between research analysts and investment banks, he required a five-year commitment from investment banks to retain independent research firms to advise their customers. In another settlement, he required mutual funds to lower their fees. Similarly, while serving as U.S. Attorney for the District of New Jersey, Chris Christie negotiated a DPA agreement with Bristol-Myers Squibb

---

[57] See James M. Doyle, "Learning from Error in American Criminal Justice," *Journal of Criminal Law and Criminology*, Vol. 100, No. 1, Winter 2010, pp. 109–148, and James M. Anderson and Paul Heaton, "How Much Difference Does the Lawyer Make? The Effect of Defense Counsel on Murder Case Outcomes," *Yale Law Journal*, Vol. 122, No. 1, October 2012, pp. 154–172 (discussing ways to improve reliability and efforts in other fields).

that resulted in the company's endowment of a chair in ethics at Seton Hall University School of Law, the law school that Christie attended.[58] In another case, prosecutors pressed the New York Racing Association to agree to install gaming machines at its racetracks, in order to raise money for the state.[59] Similarly, a settlement with MCI required the promise that MCI would add 1,600 jobs over ten years in Oklahoma.[60] Although these agreements are not typical NPAs or DPAs, they show the extent to which these agreements can vastly exceed the traditional plea agreement in scope and nexus to the offense.

Second, there is a question of institutional competence. In some cases, NPAs permit prosecutors or outside monitors (who are sometimes former federal prosecutors) to exert authority as to how the firm is run. Yet these same prosecutors or monitors rarely have business experience, a deep knowledge of the particular firms' business, or the skills necessary to manage a large firm. Prosecutors' offices are not institutionally well suited to engage in business decisionmaking or even collect the data that would be necessary for the level of oversight that some agreements entail.[61] Civil regulatory authorities may be better suited for this task because of their increased institutional knowledge of the relevant industry.[62]

---

[58] Anthony S. Barkow and Rachel E. Barkow, "Introduction," in Anthony S. Barkow and Rachel E. Barkow, eds., *Prosecutors in the Boardroom: Using Criminal Law to Regulate Corporate Conduct*, New York: New York University Press, 2011, pp. 1–10; see also Epstein, 2007.

[59] See U.S. Attorney's Office for the Eastern District of New York, "Two Former Directors of the New York Racing Association's Pari-Mutuel Department Plead Guilty to Scheme to Defraud the United States," press release, May 6, 2004, and James M. Odato, "NYRA Deal in the Works," *Albany Times Union*, December 6, 2003, p. A1.

[60] Corporate Crime Reporter, *Crime Without Conviction: The Rise of Deferred and Non Prosecution Agreements*, Washington, D.C., December 28, 2005.

[61] Arlen, 2011, pp. 76–77.

[62] Arlen, 2011, p. 79:

> [A]nalysis of the relative institutional expertise and structures of prosecutors and regulatory agencies reveals that federally mandated structural reforms are most likely to be effective if the task of designing and imposing structural reforms is left entirely to federal civil regulators, at least in the areas over which they have jurisdiction and competence.

There is also rarely any attempt to systematically measure the effectiveness of the compliance measures imposed. Although changing corporate compliance culture may be a wise goal, it is also difficult to measure. Although one can measure some kinds of compliance efforts (e.g., number of employees trained), identifying the rate of criminal activity at a firm is very difficult.

A generation ago, critics noted that undertaking large structural reform of bureaucratic institutions was not an easy task, nor one that the federal courts were particularly well suited to undertake. As Owen M. Fiss noted in 1984, "The task [of restructuring large-scale bureaucratic organizations] is enormous and our knowledge of how to restructure on-going bureaucratic organizations is limited."[63] The same critique can surely be leveled at prosecutors' offices. Although the idea of reforming a large bureaucracy may be attractive, it also may be an unrealistic goal if those who are in charge of shaping the entity's future direction do not have the experience and knowledge to successfully manage the transformation.

There is also the potential for conflicts of interest.[64] Because oversight contracts are fairly lucrative and the contracts often go to former prosecutors, these arrangements can appear unseemly at best, with prosecutors mandating that firms hire law firms that may, in turn, offer the prosecutors lucrative future employment.[65] For example, in

---

[63] Owen M. Fiss, "Against Settlement," *Yale Law Journal*, Vol. 93, No. 6, May 1984, pp. 1073–1090, p. 1083.

[64] "The Kindness of Cronies," *New York Times*, editorial, May 25, 2008.

[65] Lisa Kern Griffin, "Inside-Out Enforcement," in Anthony S. Barkow and Rachel E. Barkow, eds., *Prosecutors in the Boardroom: Using Criminal Law to Regulate Corporate Conduct*, New York: New York University Press, 2011, pp. 110–131. Griffin suggests that useful lessons might be learned from the U.S. Environmental Protection Agency's (EPA's) use of Supplemental Environmental Projects. These are projects proposed by an industry that are environmentally beneficial and, at EPA's discretion, can lead to reduced penalties. EPA permits the organization to contract with a third party but does not endorse or identify such parties in order to reduce the appearance of conflict of interest, explaining, "a close working relationship with such organizations could create the appearance that EPA is using the organization[s] as a means to indirectly manage or direct SEP funds" (John Peter Suarez, assistant administrator of the U.S. Environmental Protection Agency, "Guidance Concerning the Use of Third Parties in the Performance of Supplemental Environmental

the DPA to monitor Zimmer Holdings, the U.S. Attorney specified former Attorney General John Ashcroft's law firm as the monitor. For this work, it received $52 million. More recently, DOJ has taken efforts to prevent these conflicts. Among other reforms, a 2008 policy directive (the Morford memorandum) now requires prosecutors to notify DOJ of any DPA that specifies a particular monitor and requires the deputy attorney general to approve it.[66]

Independent monitors also raise the risk of their independence from the corporation that they are investigating. The corporations employing the monitors have an interest in advancing a narrative in which they are relatively blameless. The corporation and the outside monitor (and the prosecutor) may have an interest in identifying individual defendants to prosecute.[67] A DOJ official recently told an audience of corporate investigators that, "If you want full cooperation credit, make your extensive efforts to secure evidence of individual culpability the first thing you talk about when you walk in the door to make your presentation.[68]

But appropriately identifying the most-culpable individual defendants can be difficult, and there is some risk that less culpable individual defendants can be scapegoated.[69] Although it may be helpful and even necessary for prosecutors to enlist the corporation's assistance to identify wrongdoers, the risk of such outsourcing is the publicly

Projects (SEPs) and the Aggregation of SEP Funds," memorandum to regional counsels for regions I–X, regional enforcement managers for regions I–X, regional media division directors for regions I–X, and regional enforcement coordinators for regions I–X, December 15, 2003, part II, § B).

[66] Craig S. Morford, acting deputy attorney general, "Selection and Use of Monitors in Deferred Prosecution Agreements and Non-Prosecution Agreements with Corporations," memorandum to heads of department components and U.S. Attorneys, March 7, 2008.

[67] See Griffin, 2011, p. 122 ("The ability to deputize corporate insiders does expedite the prosecution of individual defendants and increases the total number of indictments and convictions").

[68] Aruna Viswantatha and Nate Raymond, "Holder Asks Congress for Help in Fighting Wall Street Crime," *Pittsburgh Post-Gazette*, September 18, 2014, p. A6.

[69] Griffin, 2011, pp. 113–114 (describing use of corporate investigators).

accountable prosecutors' loss of control over the process by which such wrongdoers are identified.

These agreements have also attracted criticism because they can sometimes require the dismissal of particular unindicted employees. Critics have argued that, in this instance, prosecutors are usurping the role of the board of directors, particularly for those employees who have not been indicted.[70] For those individuals who have been indicted but not convicted, there is an argument that the presumption of innocence should apply. If the corporation itself wishes to fire the individual, it should do so, but it is not clear that the prosecutor should insist on termination as a condition of an NPA. This may be outside the core competencies of the prosecutor.

In some instances, the government has encouraged firms to either terminate or sanction employees if they exercise their constitutional rights by, for example, choosing to remain silent in the face of questioning. In implementing the Thompson memorandum,[71] for example, some prosecutors have indicated that organizations will be expected to discharge or sanction individuals for exercising these rights.[72] As some critics have pointed out, the government itself would not be permitted to fire an individual for the exercise of his or her Fifth Amendment rights.[73]

Finally, these agreements can raise First Amendment questions. In New York's prosecution of brokerage houses, a condition of the settlement was that the firms would support legislation making contingent commission contracts illegal.[74] As Epstein suggests, "the problem

---

[70] For example, Epstein, 2007, pp. 53–54 (discussing practice of requiring dismissal of employees as condition for NPA and how it can encourage board to fire a CEO).

[71] In particular, the clause indicating that cooperation may not be found if the organization is supporting "culpable employees and agents . . . through retaining the employees without sanction for their misconduct" (Thompson, 2003, pp. 7–8).

[72] R. William Ide III, *ABA Presidential Task Force on the Attorney–Client Privilege*, August 2006, pp. 15–16.

[73] *Gardner v. Broderick*, 392 U.S. 273 (1968) (finding that a state may not discharge its employee solely for refusing to waive constitutional right against self-incrimination).

[74] See Epstein, 2007.

with this condition is that it was used to reshape the public debate over important issues by forcing a criminal defendant to take sides on an issue that does not represent his or her views."[75]

## Conclusion

In this section, we reviewed the recent history of DOJ policy on organizational prosecutions and the rise of DPAs and NPAs. The Sentencing Reform Act of 1984 and the Federal Sentencing Guidelines for Organizations of 1991 dramatically increased the importance of compliance programs and emphasized the goal of structurally reforming the corporation. But the restructuring was initially a requirement of probation and therefore occurred only after a corporation was convicted. Over time, however, the importance of compliance programs and restructuring moved up in the criminal process and became a criterion on which a decision to prosecute was made.

In the wake of the Arthur Andersen prosecution, both corporate directors and prosecutors drew lessons that minimized subsequent trials. For directors, the fate of Andersen highlighted the potentially firm-ending risks of taking a case to trial. For prosecutors, the end of Andersen and its effect on thousands of innocent employees and stakeholders highlighted the potential collateral damage that aggressively pursuing a corporate prosecution can entail. Perhaps as a result of this renewed appreciation of the downsides of trial, NPAs and DPAs became much more popular. These allowed prosecutors to accomplish their objective of reforming the corporation without the expense, delay, and risk of trial. For corporations, NPAs and DPAs permit the corporation to avoid indictment and the substantial collateral consequences that may result.

However, the increased use of DPAs and NPAs also had substantial disadvantages. Some of the terms of NPAs and DPAs have had limited nexus to the offense and have included terms that raise concerns. These include the firms adopting particular political positions or

[75] Epstein, 2007, p. 53.

hiring particular monitors. More generally, they represent the partial privatization and outsourcing of an important aspect of the criminal justice system that has historically been considered a core government function.

Our review of this recent history provides context for the quantitative analysis of corporate prosecutions in the next chapter.

CHAPTER FOUR

# Trends in Prosecutions of Corporations and Individuals

We turn here to an analysis of available data to provide evidence on how the focus of criminal law in the corporate context has changed from prosecuting offenders to encouraging the corporation itself to police misconduct. Specifically, we look at federal prosecution trends concerning corporations and white-collar criminal offenses, trends in DPAs and NPAs, and trends in debarment. We use multiple sources of data for our analysis, which sometimes conflict but overall show a consistent theme. (See Chapter One for details about our data sources.)

The notion that there is a recent shift to using criminal law to reform offending corporations from within is supported by an array of empirical evidence that shows that DPAs and NPAs, as well as debarments, have been on the rise. This evidence also demonstrates that, contrary to some perceptions, prosecutions of corporate actors are declining. With the exceptions of the application of SOX and the FCPA, we found that prosecutions of corporations and corporate-related offenses have been declining since the mid-1990s.

## Overall Trend: Declining Prosecutions

First, the number of corporations convicted in federal courts appears to have declined in the past decade, while use of DPAs and NPAs has increased. Second, there has been an overall decline in prosecuting corporate offenses since the turn of the century through the 2008 financial crisis.

Using both Sentencing Commission data and Garrett's database (discussed in Chapter One), we find that there has been a decrease in the number of firms convicted in federal courts during the past decade. As shown in Figure 4.1, the Sentencing Commission depicts an unstable decrease, whereas Garrett's data depict a more gradual decrease. Nonetheless, fewer firms were prosecuted and convicted by the end of the decade than in 2000. Although the time periods covered by each source of data are different and the methods of compiling the data are slightly different, the overall trends from both sources of data are very similar. This gives us some confidence that the trend we are observing in the data reflects an actual underlying decline in the number of convicted corporations.

**Figure 4.1**
**Corporations Convicted in Federal Courts**

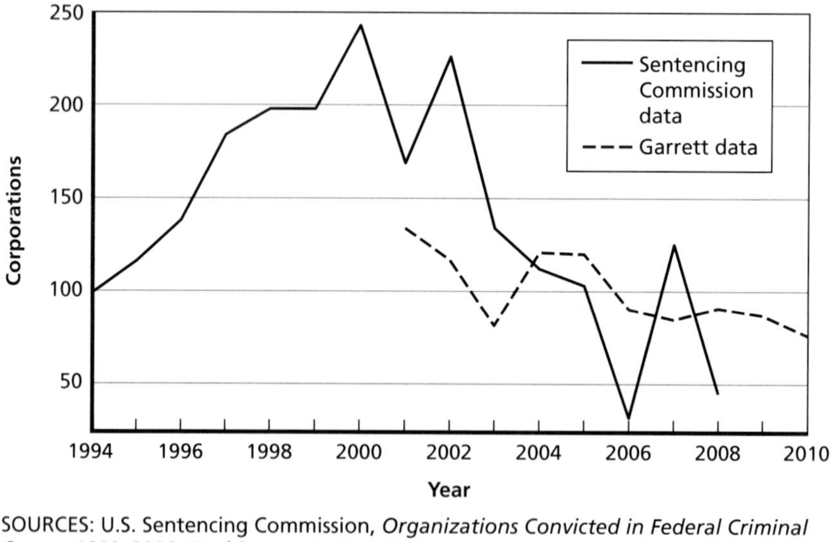


SOURCES: U.S. Sentencing Commission, *Organizations Convicted in Federal Criminal Courts, 1999–2008*, Washington, D.C., 1999; Brandon L. Garrett and Jon Ashley, "Federal Organizational Plea Agreements," Charlottesville, Va.: University of Virginia School of Law, undated.

RAND *RR412-4.1*

## Convictions and Firm Size

Numerically, small corporations faced the most convictions. As Figure 4.2 shows, midsized firms had the second-most firms facing convictions. Large corporations, on the other hand, faced the fewest convictions. This is not surprising given that there are fewer large corporations in the United States than small firms.

However, when examining trends in the *percentage* of firms of different sizes that have been convicted, the situation reverses. A greater percentage of large firms were convicted in federal courts than midsized and small firms, respectively (see Figure 4.2). Thus, in our sample of convicted firms, large firms were more likely than smaller ones to experience prosecutions and convictions.

## Prosecution of Individuals Alongside Convicted Corporations

As was discussed in Chapter Two, corporations can be vicariously liable for their employees' behavior. However, there is no requirement that corporations always be subject to prosecution for criminal acts committed by their employees or vice versa. Accordingly, in the United States, prosecutors are given a substantial amount of discretion on whether to bring charges against a corporation or an individual defendant.

Data from the Sentencing Commission show an overall increase in the number of convictions involving both corporations and individuals guilty of the same offense. As Figure 4.3 shows, sentencing individuals alongside corporations appears more prevalent in 2008 than in 1994. This is consistent with the changes in DOJ policy (discussed in Chapter Three) that emphasized individual prosecutions.

## Differences in the Enforcement of Civil and Criminal Law

The use of either civil or criminal law over the other appears to depend on the type of legal matter. The data from the *Federal Court Cases:*

**Figure 4.2**
**Conviction Trends for Firms of Different Sizes**

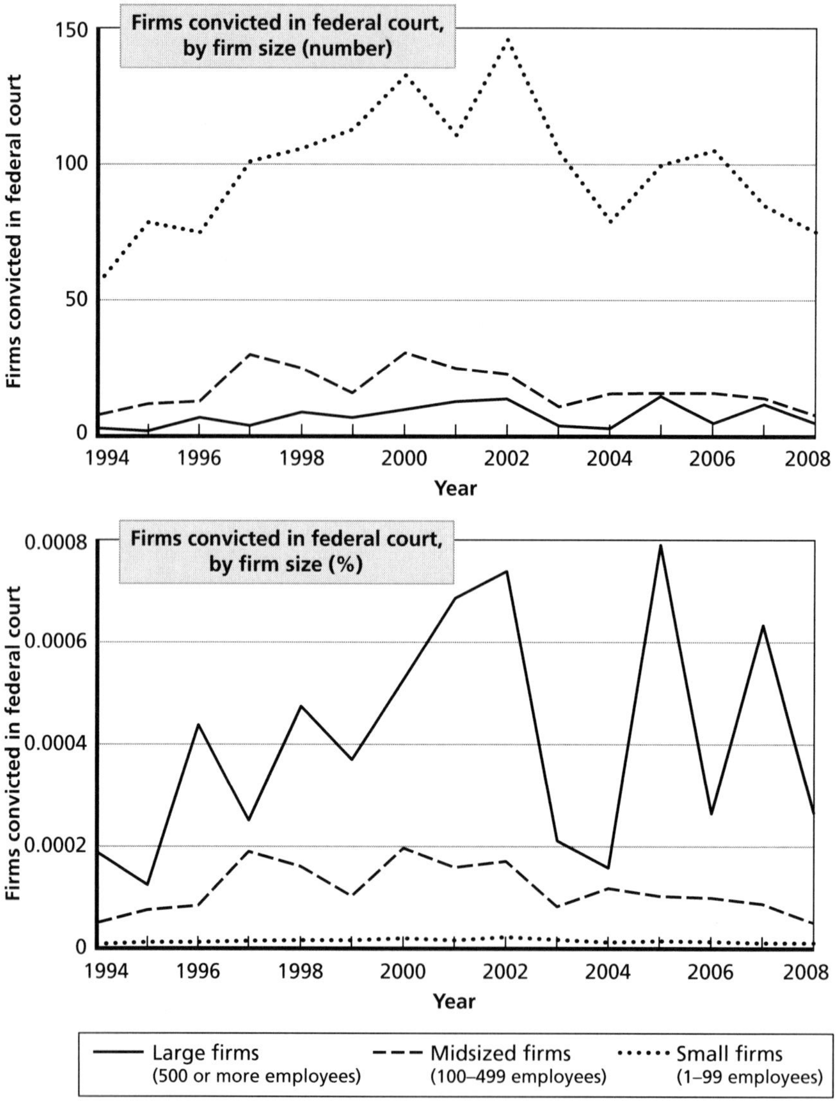


SOURCE: U.S. Sentencing Commission, 1999.
RAND *RR412-4.2*

**Figure 4.3**
**Number of Corporations Sentenced Alongside Individual Codefendants**

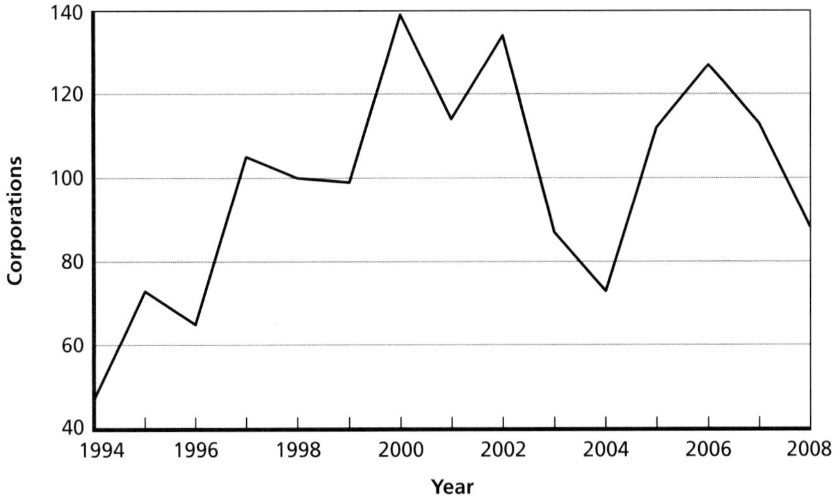


SOURCE: U.S. Sentencing Commission, 1999.
RAND *RR412-4.3*

*Integrated Data Base*[1] allows us to compare trends between the enforcement of civil and criminal laws governing specific areas, such as securities and commodities or antitrust.

Regarding security- and commodity-related offenses, the United States appears to pursue civil sanctions more often than criminal, as shown in Figure 4.4. In contrast, more prosecutions for antitrust matters appear to take place than civil suits brought by the U.S. government.

## Deferred Prosecution Agreements and Nonprosecution Agreements

The decrease in the number of firms convicted coincides with a striking increase in the number of DPAs and NPAs reached by prosecutors with firms suspected of criminal behavior, as shown in Figure 4.5. Although DOJ used DPAs and NPAs during the 1990s to a limited extent, it

1 Federal Judicial Center, 2011.

**Figure 4.4**
**Trends in Criminal and Civil Prosecutions**

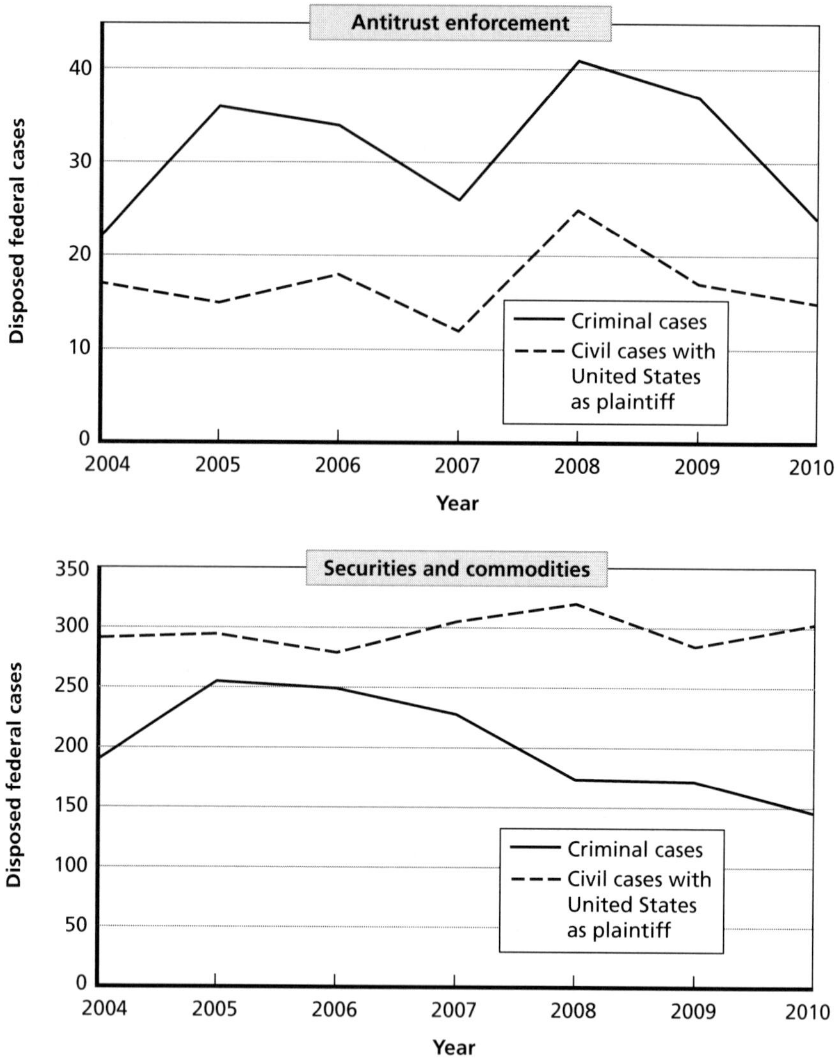


SOURCE: Federal Judicial Center, 2011.
RAND *RR412-4.4*

**Figure 4.5**
**Deferred-Prosecution and Nonprosecution Agreements from 1992 to 2010**

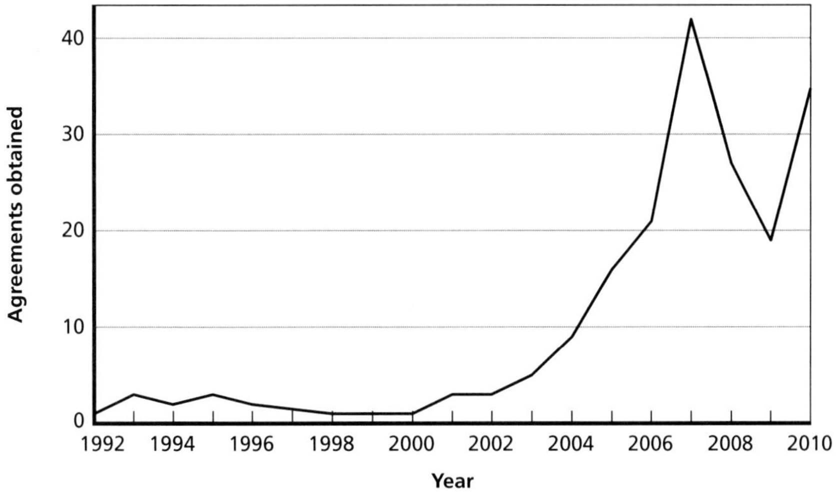


SOURCE: Garrett and Ashley, undated.
RAND *RR412-4.5*

significantly increased their use beginning around 2003. From 1992 to 2002, DOJ reached only 20 agreements.[2] From 2003 to 2010, however, it reached 174 agreements.[3] Although we cannot be certain that a causal relationship exists, it is notable that the jump in DPA and NPAs occurs immediately following the collapse of Arthur Andersen discussed in Chapter Three.

Precisely because the cases are diverted before indictment, they are difficult to study. In fact, few have studied them empirically. The first empirical study examined trends in deferred prosecutions from 1993 to 2007.[4] Garrett found a dramatic increase in DPAs and NPAs following the Thompson memorandum that encouraged prosecutors to seek pretrial diversion for potential corporate defendants and encour-

---

[2] Brandon L. Garrett and Jon Ashley, "Federal Organizational Prosecution Agreements," last updated October 27, 2014.

[3] Garrett and Ashley, 2014.

[4] Garrett, 2007.

aged both DPAs and NPAs.[5] Garrett compiled his data from the DOJ and U.S. Attorneys' Office websites, where they have publicly posted DPAs and NPAs since 2003.[6]

Prior to 2003, DOJ did not publicly release all agreements. Garrett was able to locate 13 DPAs and NPAs from reasonably available sources, such as news articles.[7] In contrast, he found 35 agreements from 2003 to 2007.[8] In addition to the increase in use of these agreements, Garrett found that agreements post-2003 included more-comprehensive compliance programs, long-term use of independent monitors, and an increase in penalty fines.[9] The agreements prior to 2003 that Garrett was able to locate had short-term use of independent monitors, few compliance programs, and fewer penalty fines.[10] We discuss the development of these agreements in more detail in the next chapter.

## White-Collar Offenses

Prosecution trends of white-collar crime can be a potential metric for the enforcement of illegal corporate behavior. As Figure 4.6 illustrates, the prosecution of white-collar offenses gradually declined from the mid-1990s until about 2006, when they gradually began to increase. Although white-collar offenses encompass crimes committed in the corporate context, the category is broader and includes a wide range of fraudulent conduct that does not necessarily occur in the corporate

---

5 Garrett, 2007, p. 894.

6 Garrett, 2007, p. 938.

7 Garrett, 2007. Garrett admits that he is not confident that he has located all DPAs and NPAs obtained prior to 2003.

8 Garrett, 2007.

9 Garrett, 2007, pp. 901, 938–957.

10 Garrett, 2007, pp. 938–957. Garrett hoped that his data would serve as a foundation for prosecutors, scholars, and others who may be interested in assessing these agreements' effectiveness (Garrett, 2007, p. 937). To date, however, no study has attempted to assess their effectiveness or their costs to the targeted corporations.

**Figure 4.6**
**Federal Prosecutions of White-Collar Crimes**

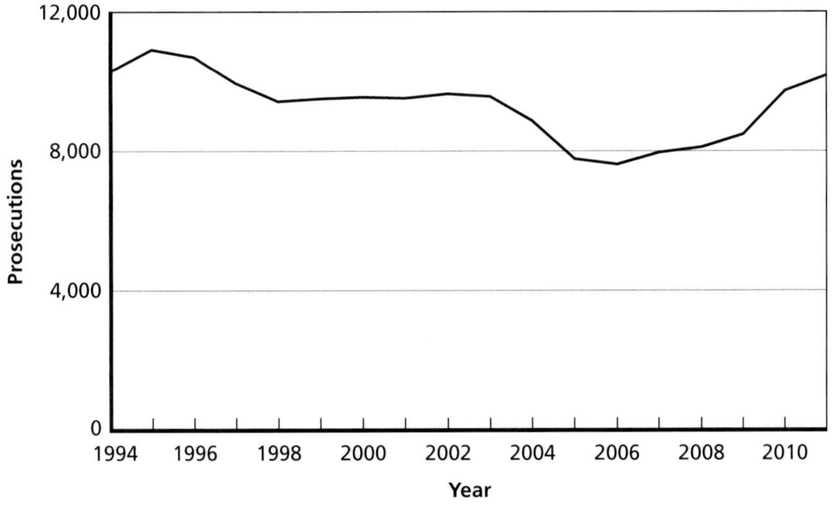


SOURCE: TRAC, undated (a).
RAND *RR412-4.6*

context. Accordingly, we look to specific prosecution trends of offenses that are more relevant to the context of corporate criminal liability.

A consistent theme we found in the data for the past century has been a decrease in prosecutions. Unfortunately, the data used from EOUSA do not indicate whether a defendant is a corporation or an individual.

The EOUSA database categorizes and codes offenses into groups, such as antitrust or securities fraud. TRACFED allowed us to match prosecution data and create additional data sets to substantiate our findings. Thus, we were able to compare and contrast, side by side, prosecution trends among the following types of corporate offenses: (1) securities fraud; (2) lending-institution fraud; (3) marketing and commodities fraud; (4) antitrust offenses; (5) commerce and trade offenses; (6) embezzlement of lending, credit, or insurance institutions; (7) hazardous-waste disposal; and (8) fair-labor offenses.

Securities fraud involves individuals or corporations who commit some form of fraud involving securities, such as falsifying required periodic disclosures to the SEC. As Figure 4.7 shows, data from both EOUSA and TRACFED show a significant decline in prosecution activity since 2000.[11]

---

[11] Although both sets of data show a decline in prosecution activity leading up to the 2008 financial crisis, data from EOUSA do not show as dramatic a decrease in referrals from investigative agencies as TRACFED data do (Garrett, 2007). This discrepancy may result from any of several reasons. For instance, TRACFED's definition of securities fraud encompasses many more federal statutes, whereas data from EOUSA contain only fraud offenses arising from the Securities Exchange Act of 1934. Moreover, although data from EOUSA and TRACFED likely come from the same source (the U.S. Attorneys' LIONS and Central System File), different organizations collect, process, and compile the databases. Thus, some information may have been lost or manipulated during the differing processes used. On a final note, TRACFED's data, which are more recent, show a slight increase in prosecutorial activity in this area since 2008 (Garrett, 2007). Note that prosecutorial activity differs from prosecution. A prosecution involves the filing of a charge against an individual or organization. One of the developments we discuss is an increase in prosecutorial activity that does not result in the filing of a charge (e.g., negotiating a DPA or NPA). This is not really a prosecution.

The sources for Figures 4.7 through 4.14 are BJS, *Federal Justice Statistics Program: Defendants in Federal Criminal Cases: Terminated, 1994*, Ann Arbor, Mich.: Inter-university Consortium for Political and Social Research, March 8, 2011a; BJS, *Federal Justice Statistics Program: Defendants in Federal Criminal Cases: Terminated, 1995*, Ann Arbor, Mich.: Inter-university Consortium for Political and Social Research, March 8, 2011b; BJS, *Federal Justice Statistics Program: Defendants in Federal Criminal Cases: Terminated, 1996*, Ann Arbor, Mich.: Inter-university Consortium for Political and Social Research, March 8, 2011c; BJS, *Federal Justice Statistics Program: Defendants in Federal Criminal Cases: Terminated, 1997*, Ann Arbor, Mich.: Inter-university Consortium for Political and Social Research, March 8, 2011d; BJS, *Federal Justice Statistics Program: Defendants in Federal Criminal Cases: Terminated, 1998*, Ann Arbor, Mich.: Inter-university Consortium for Political and Social Research, March 8, 2011e; BJS, *Federal Justice Statistics Program: Defendants in Federal Criminal Cases: Terminated, 1999*, Ann Arbor, Mich.: Inter-university Consortium for Political and Social Research, March 8, 2011f; BJS, *Federal Justice Statistics Program: Defendants in Federal Criminal Cases: Terminated, 2000*, Ann Arbor, Mich.: Inter-university Consortium for Political and Social Research, March 8, 2011g; BJS, *Federal Justice Statistics Program: Defendants in Federal Criminal Cases: Terminated, 2001*, Ann Arbor, Mich.: Inter-university Consortium for Political and Social Research, March 8, 2011h; BJS, *Federal Justice Statistics Program: Defendants in Federal Criminal Cases: Terminated, 2002*, Ann Arbor, Mich.: Inter-university Consortium for Political and Social Research, March 8, 2011i; BJS, *Federal Justice Statistics Program: Defendants in Federal Criminal Cases: Terminated, 2003*, Ann Arbor, Mich.: Inter-university Consortium for Political and Social Research, March 8, 2011j; BJS, *Federal Justice Statistics Program: Defendants in Federal Criminal Cases: Terminated, 2004*, Ann Arbor, Mich.: Inter-university Consortium for Political and Social Research, March 8, 2011k; BJS, *Federal Justice Statistics Program: Defendants in Federal Criminal Cases:*

**Figure 4.7**
**Prosecution Data on Securities Fraud**

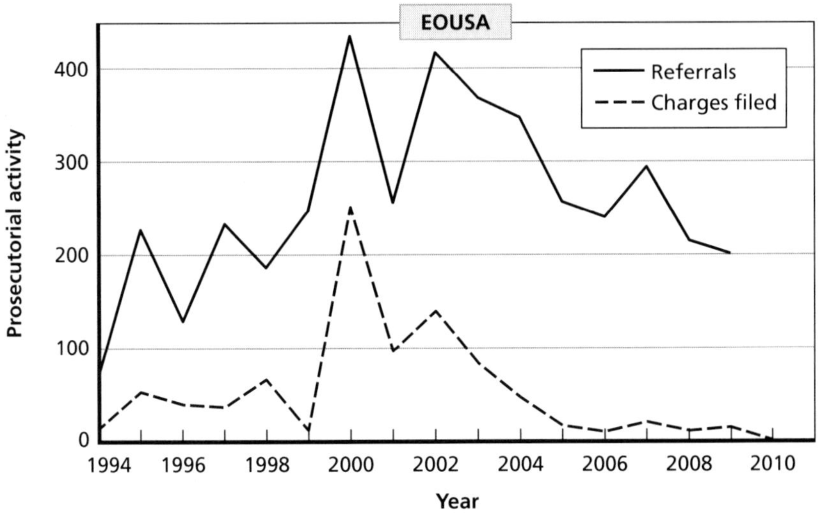


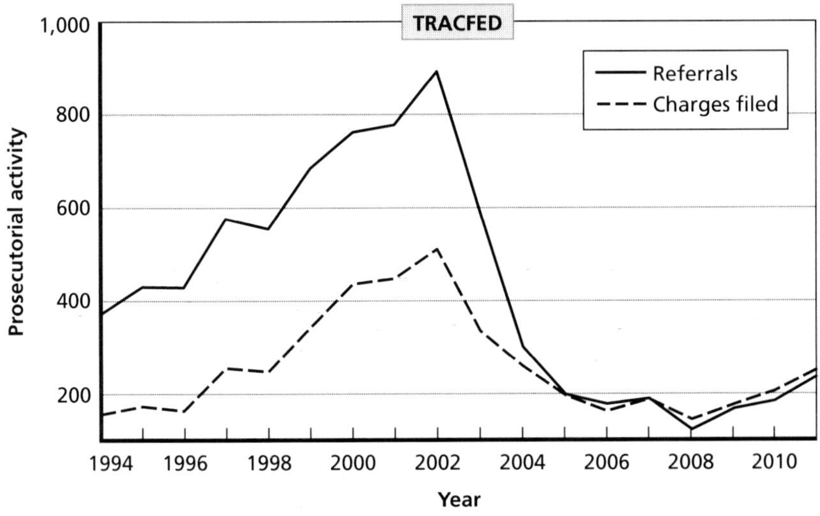


RAND *RR412-4.7*

---

*Terminated, 2005*, Ann Arbor, Mich.: Inter-university Consortium for Political and Social Research, March 8, 2011l; BJS, *Federal Justice Statistics Program: Defendants in Federal Criminal Cases: Terminated, 2006*, Ann Arbor, Mich.: Inter-university Consortium for Political

The most common offense in this category involves overvaluing property or securities with the purpose of influencing financial institu-

---

and Social Research, March 8, 2011m; BJS, *Federal Justice Statistics Program: Defendants in Federal Criminal Cases: Terminated, 2007*, Ann Arbor, Mich.: Inter-university Consortium for Political and Social Research, March 8, 2011n; BJS, *Federal Justice Statistics Program: Defendants in Federal Criminal Cases: Terminated, 2008*, Ann Arbor, Mich.: Inter-university Consortium for Political and Social Research, March 8, 2011o; BJS, *Federal Justice Statistics Program: Suspects in Federal Criminal Matters Concluded, 1994*, Ann Arbor, Mich.: Inter-university Consortium for Political and Social Research, March 8, 2011p; BJS, *Federal Justice Statistics Program: Suspects in Federal Criminal Matters Concluded, 1995*, Ann Arbor, Mich.: Inter-university Consortium for Political and Social Research, March 8, 2011q; BJS, *Federal Justice Statistics Program: Suspects in Federal Criminal Matters Concluded, 1996*, Ann Arbor, Mich.: Inter-university Consortium for Political and Social Research, March 8, 2011r; BJS, *Federal Justice Statistics Program: Suspects in Federal Criminal Matters Concluded, 1997*, Ann Arbor, Mich.: Inter-university Consortium for Political and Social Research, March 8, 2011s; BJS, *Federal Justice Statistics Program: Suspects in Federal Criminal Matters Concluded, 1998*, Ann Arbor, Mich.: Inter-university Consortium for Political and Social Research, March 8, 2011t; BJS, *Federal Justice Statistics Program: Suspects in Federal Criminal Matters Concluded, 1999*, Ann Arbor, Mich.: Inter-university Consortium for Political and Social Research, March 8, 2011u; BJS, *Federal Justice Statistics Program: Suspects in Federal Criminal Matters Concluded, 2000*, Ann Arbor, Mich.: Inter-university Consortium for Political and Social Research, March 8, 2011v; BJS, *Federal Justice Statistics Program: Suspects in Federal Criminal Matters Concluded, 2001*, Ann Arbor, Mich.: Inter-university Consortium for Political and Social Research, March 8, 2011w; BJS, *Federal Justice Statistics Program: Suspects in Federal Criminal Matters Concluded, 2002*, Ann Arbor, Mich.: Inter-university Consortium for Political and Social Research, March 8, 2011x; BJS, *Federal Justice Statistics Program: Suspects in Federal Criminal Matters Concluded, 2003*, Ann Arbor, Mich.: Inter-university Consortium for Political and Social Research, March 8, 2011y; BJS, *Federal Justice Statistics Program: Suspects in Federal Criminal Matters Concluded, 2004*, Ann Arbor, Mich.: Inter-university Consortium for Political and Social Research, March 8, 2011z; BJS, *Federal Justice Statistics Program: Suspects in Federal Criminal Matters Concluded, 2005*, Ann Arbor, Mich.: Inter-university Consortium for Political and Social Research, March 8, 2011aa; BJS, *Federal Justice Statistics Program: Suspects in Federal Criminal Matters Concluded, 2006*, Ann Arbor, Mich.: Inter-university Consortium for Political and Social Research, March 8, 2011bb; BJS, *Federal Justice Statistics Program: Suspects in Federal Criminal Matters Concluded, 2007*, Ann Arbor, Mich.: Inter-university Consortium for Political and Social Research, March 8, 2011cc; BJS, *Federal Justice Statistics Program: Suspects in Federal Criminal Matters Concluded, 2008*, Ann Arbor, Mich.: Inter-university Consortium for Political and Social Research, March 8, 2011dd; BJS, *Federal Justice Statistics Program: Defendants in Federal Criminal Cases: Terminated, 2009*, Ann Arbor, Mich.: Inter-university Consortium for Political and Social Research, June 3, 2011gg; BJS, *Federal Justice Statistics Program: Suspects in Federal Criminal Matters Concluded, 2009*, Ann Arbor, Mich.: Inter-university Consortium for Political and Social Research, June 3, 2011hh; TRAC, undated (a).

tions, such as a credit union or a Federal Reserve Bank.[12] Data from both U.S. Attorneys' Offices and TRACFED depict a steady decline in prosecution activity since the mid-1990s through the 2008 financial crisis. Figure 4.8 shows that data from EOUSA differ from TRACFED data in that the former show that there are far more referrals for prosecution from investigative agencies than charges filed.[13] In contrast, TRACFED data show that, since 2000, referrals have nearly matched the number of charges filed. Interpreting this trend with TRACFED, however, is difficult because data from EOUSA do not substantiate it.

Marketing and commodity-credit fraud pertains to making false statements or overvaluing securities to influence the Commodity Credit Corporation,[14] a government-owned corporation created in 1933 to "stabilize, support, and protect farm income and prices."[15] Like securities and lending-institution fraud, data from both TRACFED and EOUSA show a spike in prosecution activity in the mid-1990s, followed by a sharp decline (see Figure 4.9).

Although past studies that examined earlier periods found few discernible trends regarding antitrust enforcement,[16] we found a decline in DOJ antitrust prosecutions since the mid-1990s. Figure 4.10 shows this decline.

Commerce and trade offenses concern the conversion of trade secrets of products placed in interstate commerce.[17] As Figure 4.11

---

[12] U.S. Code, Title 18, Crimes and Criminal Procedure, Part I, Crimes, Chapter 47, Fraud and False Statements, Section 1014, Loan and Credit Applications Generally—Renewals and Discounts, Crop Insurance, 1976.

[13] A referral for prosecution represents a case investigated by an agency and referred to the U.S. Attorneys' Office for prosecution.

[14] 15 U.S.C. § 714m (1976).

[15] Public Law 80-806, Commodity Credit Corporation Charter Act of 1948, June 29, 1948.

[16] Richard A. Posner, "A Statistical Study of Antitrust Enforcement," *Journal of Law and Economics*, Vol. 13, No. 2, October 1970, pp. 365–419, p. 367; Joseph C. Gallo, Kenneth Dau-Schmidt, Joseph L. Craycraft, and Charles J. Parker, "Department of Justice Antitrust Enforcement, 1995–1997: An Empirical Study," *Review of Industrial Organization*, Vol. 17, 2000, pp. 75–133, pp. 76–77.

[17] U.S. Code, Title 18, Crimes and Criminal Procedure, Part I, Crimes, Chapter 90, Protection of Trade Secrets, Section 1832, Theft of Trade Secrets, 1976.

**Figure 4.8**
**Federal Prosecutions for Lending Fraud**

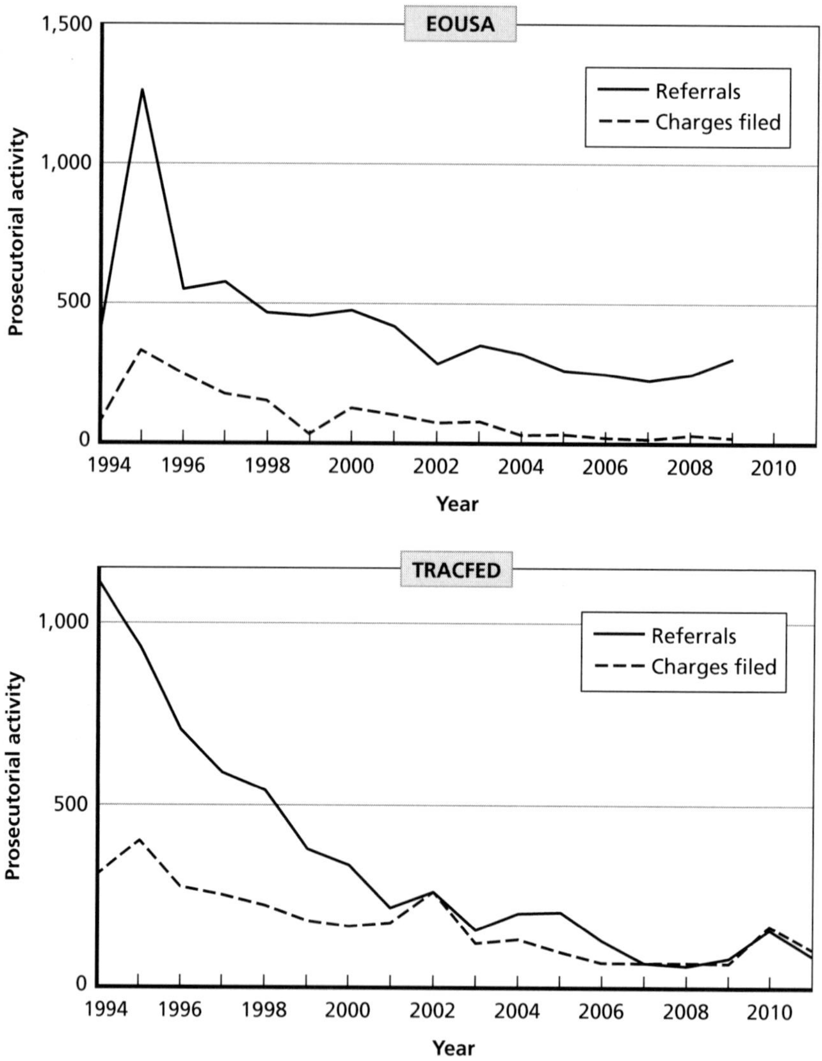


RAND *RR412-4.8*

**Figure 4.9**
**Federal Prosecutions for Marketing and Commodity-Credit Fraud**

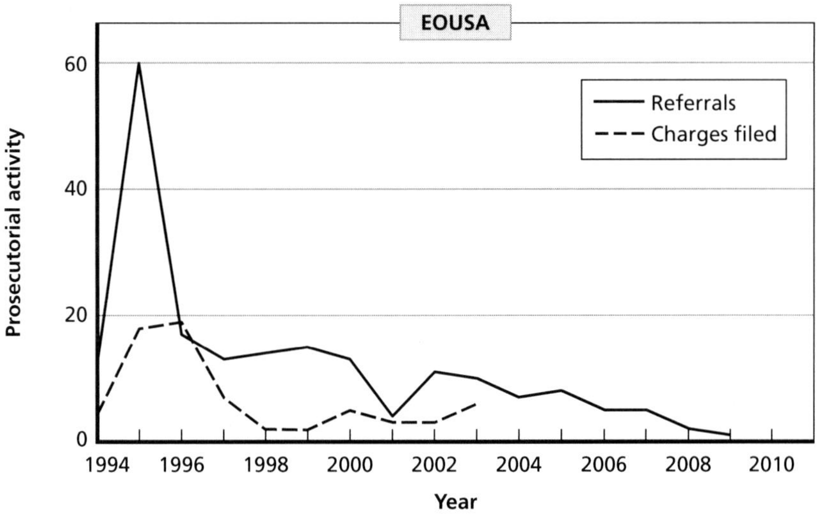


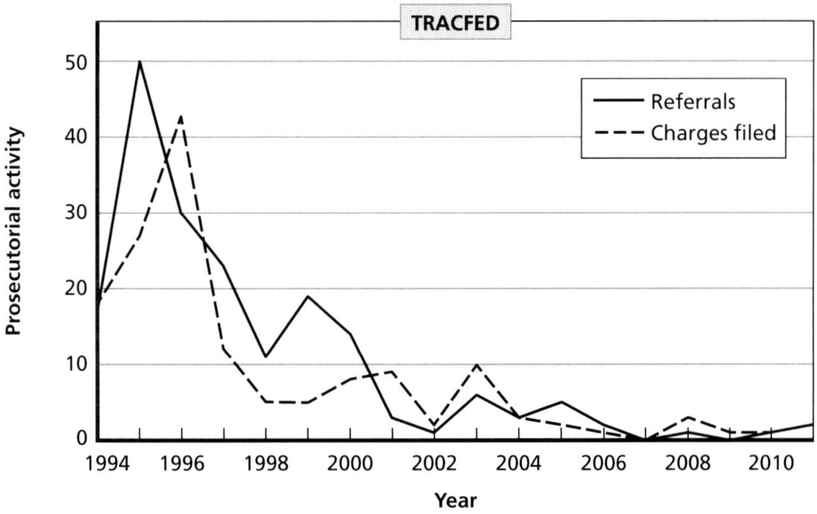


RAND *RR412-4.9*

**Figure 4.10**
**Federal Prosecutions for Antitrust Offenses**

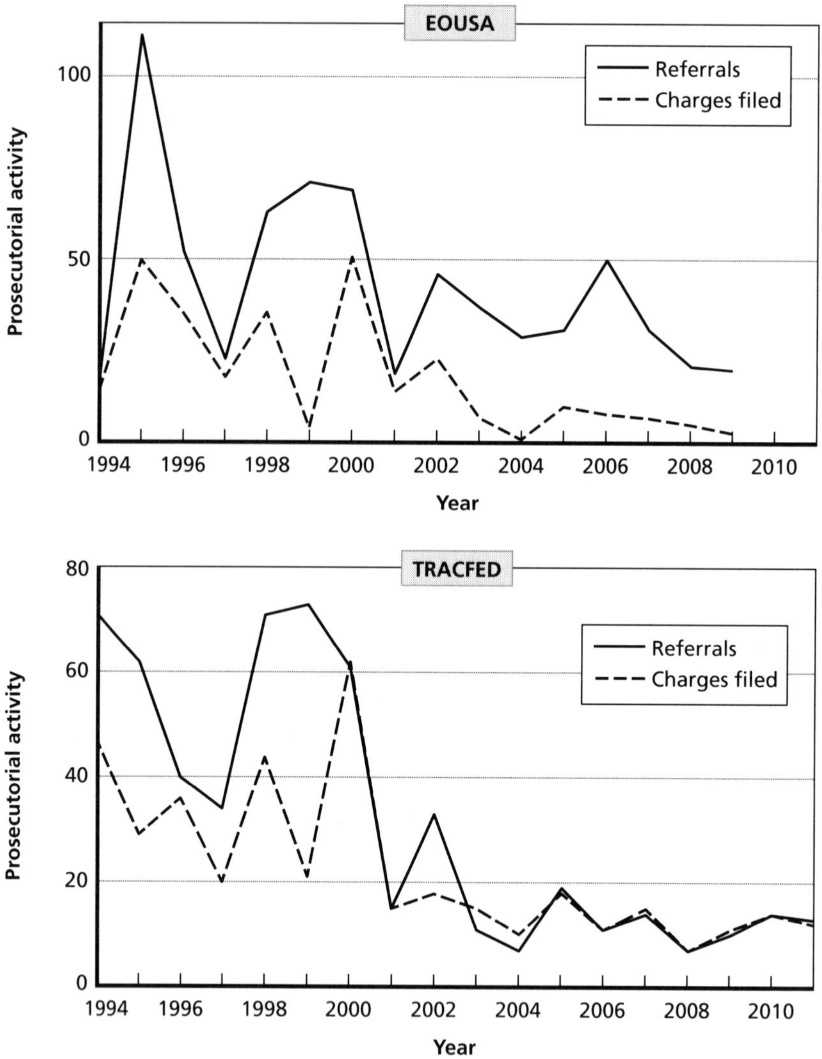


RAND *RR412-4.10*

shows, prosecutions of these types of offenses, like the other prosecutions discussed above, have declined in the past decade.

**Figure 4.11**
**Federal Prosecutions for Commerce and Trade Offenses**

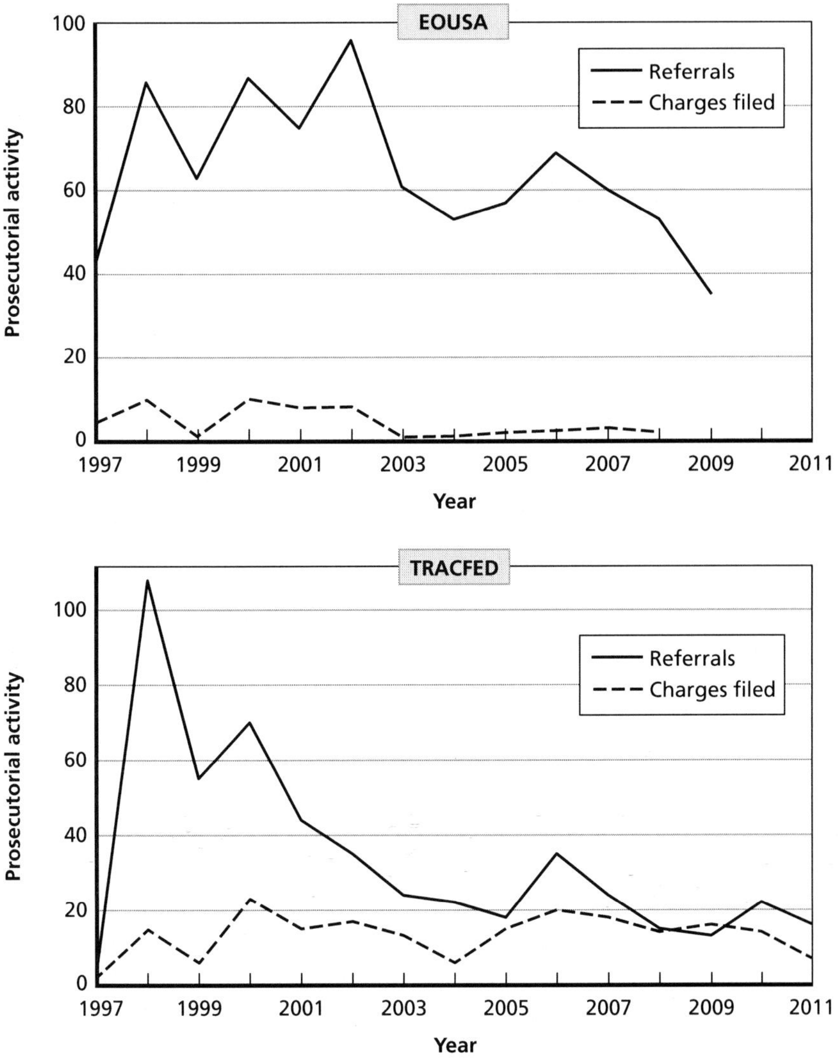


RAND *RR412-4.11*

Embezzlement related to lending, credit, or insurance institutions pertains to employees who embezzle money from U.S. financial institutions.[18] Referrals and the number of charges filed by U.S. Attorneys have declined since a mid-1990s spike in prosecution activity, as shown in Figure 4.12. This spike was probably related to the aftermath of the savings and loan crises of the late 1980s and early 1990s.

Numerous corporations handle hazardous waste and are therefore subject to relevant environmental laws. Accordingly, we included analysis of prosecution trends for hazardous-waste disposal. As shown in Figure 4.13, these offenses have also seen a decline in prosecution activity from the mid-1990s to the present because both referrals from investigative agencies and prosecutions have declined steadily in this period.

Fair-labor-standard offenses stem from violating the Fair Labor Standards Act, which provides a minimum amount of protections for wage employees, as well as sanctions to employers or unions that falsify labor reports to the Secretary of Labor.[19] Referrals and prosecutions of these offenses have also declined in the past decade, as shown in Figure 4.14; however, the baseline rate of prosecutorial activity was relatively low.

## Important Exceptions: Sarbanes-Oxley and Foreign Corrupt Practices Act

Although the evidence shows a decrease in prosecuting corporate-related offenses in the past decade, certain laws have received more attention than others. In particular, we find that prosecutions under provisions of SOX and the FCPA have been on the rise.

Using the Federal Court Cases Integrated Database, we found a steady increase in the number of defendants convicted under SOX

[18] U.S. Code, Title 18, Crimes and Criminal Procedure, Part I, Crimes, Chapter 31, Embezzlement and Theft, Section 657, Lending, Credit and Insurance Institutions, 1976.

[19] Public Law 75-718, Fair Labor Standards Act of 1938, June 25, 1938; U.S. Code, Title 29, Labor, Chapter 8, Fair Labor Standards, Section 215, Prohibited Acts—Prima Facie Evidence, 1976; U.S. Code, Title 29, Labor, Chapter 11, Labor-Management Reporting and Disclosure Procedure, Subchapter III, Reporting by Labor Organizations, Officers and Employees of Labor Organizations, and Employers, Section 433, Report of Employers, 1976.

**Figure 4.12**
**Federal Prosecutions for Embezzlement from Lending, Credit, or Insurance Institutions**

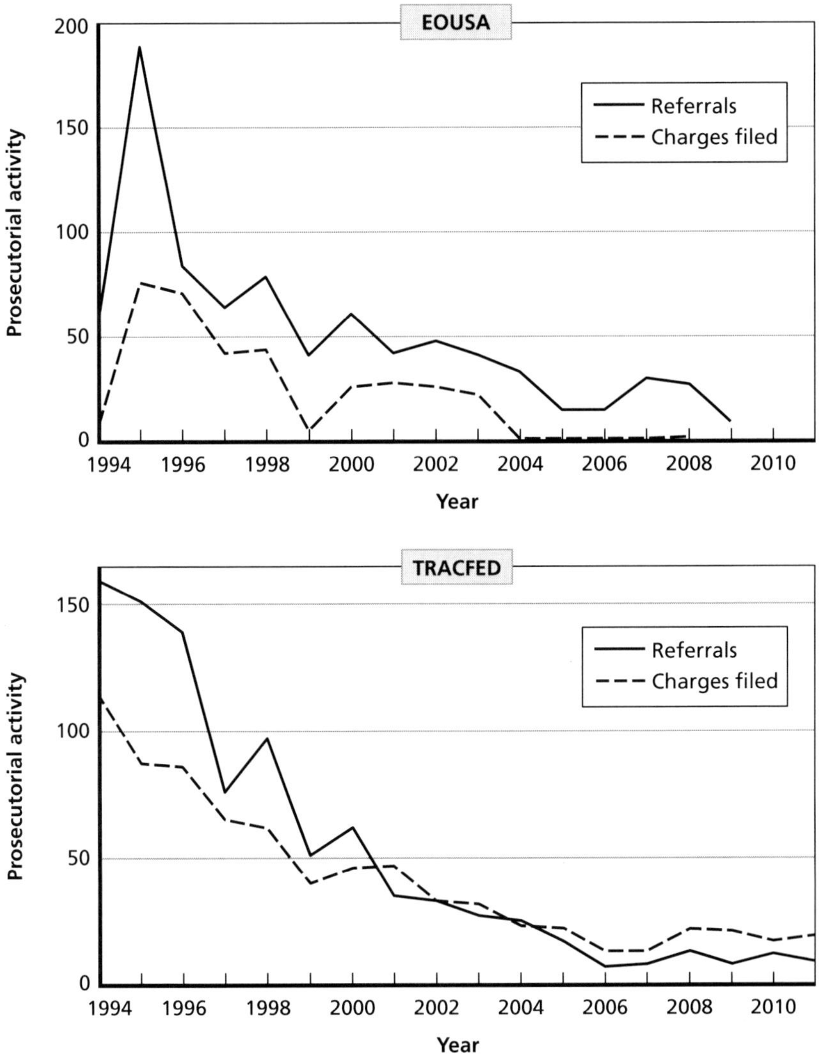


RAND *RR412-4.12*

**Figure 4.13**
**Federal Prosecutions for Hazardous Waste–Related Offenses**

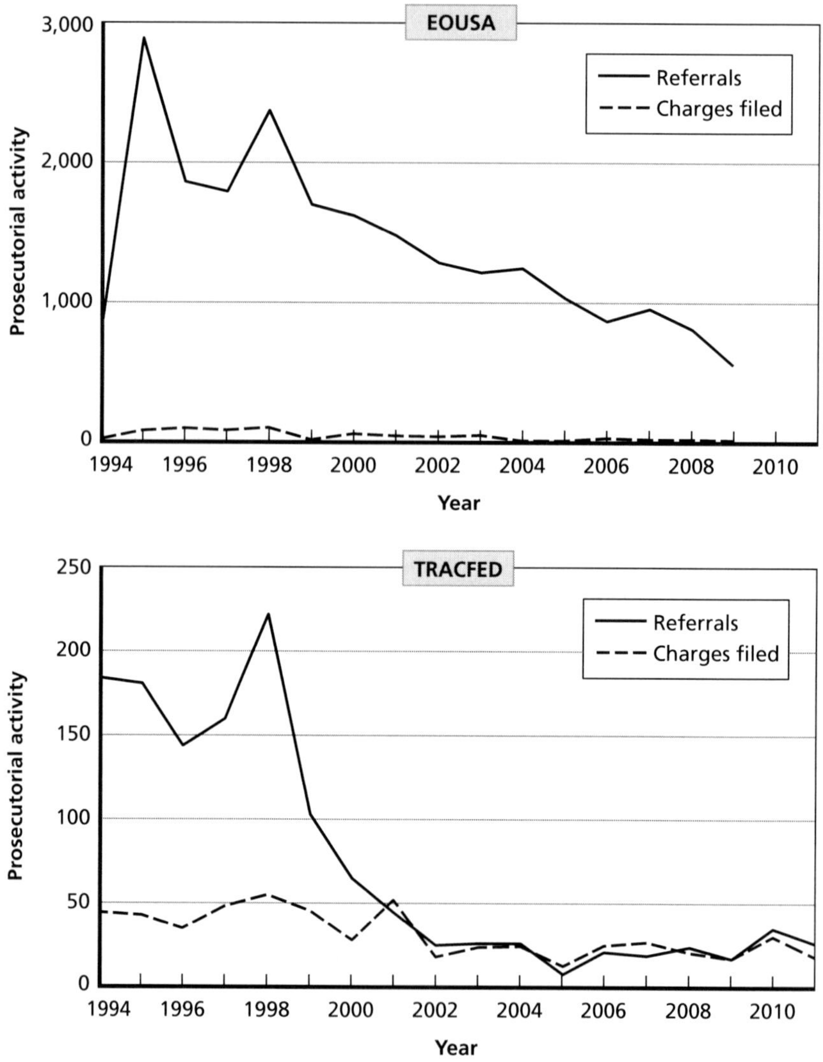


RAND *RR412-4.13*

**Figure 4.14**
**Federal Prosecutions for Fair Labor Standards Act Offenses**

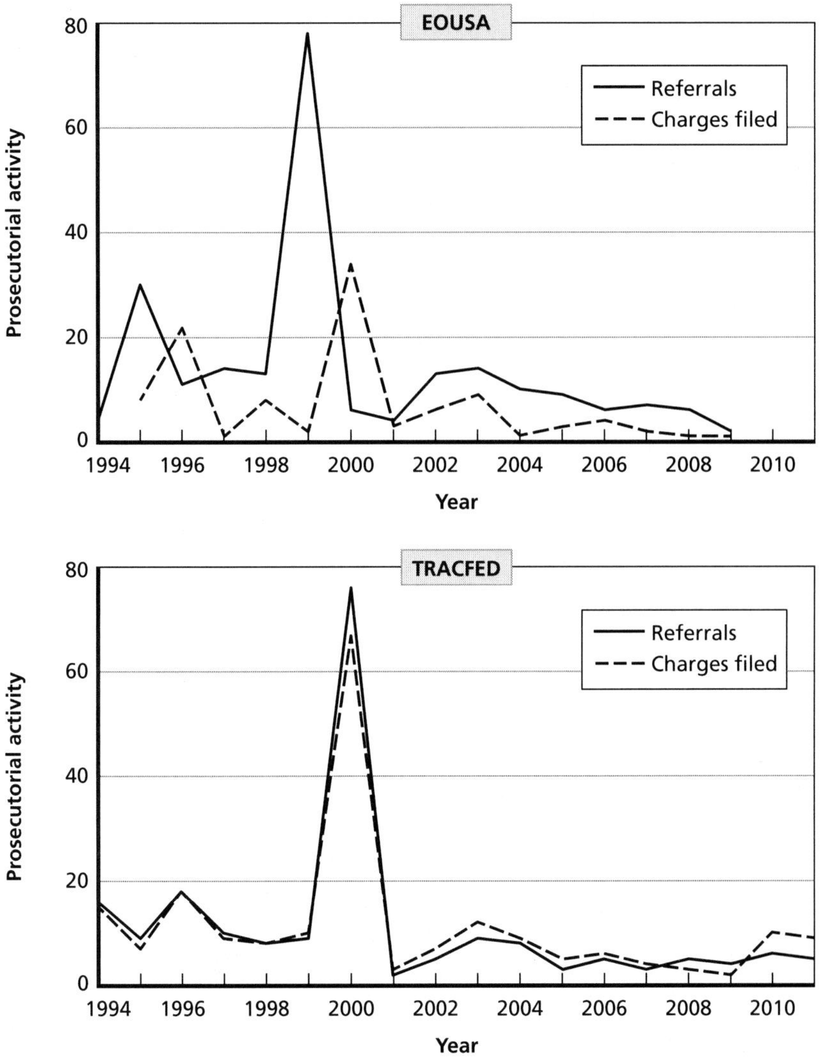


RAND *RR412-4.14*

**Figure 4.15**
**Enforcement of Sarbanes-Oxley Criminal Provisions**

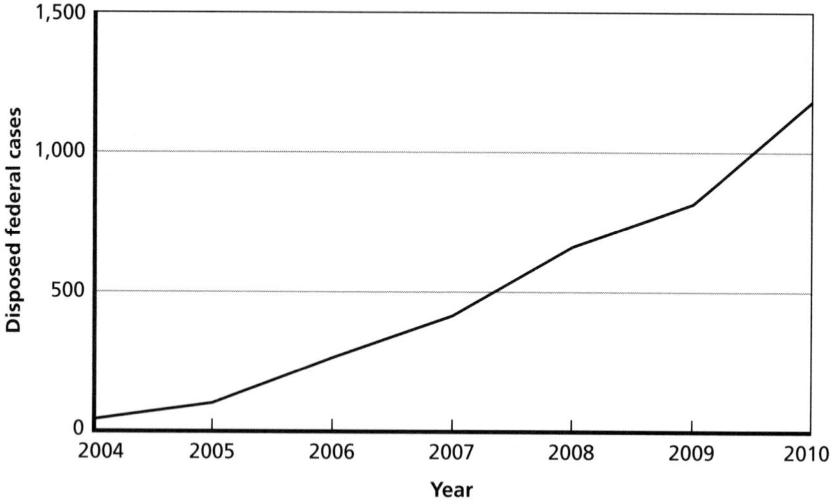


SOURCE: Federal Judicial Center, 2011.
RAND *RR412-4.15*

since 2004 (see Figure 4.15). We measured convictions by the number of SOX criminal provisions under which defendants were convicted.[20] In the data since 2004, we found 3,476 defendants convicted under at least one of SOX's criminal provisions. In short, it appears that pros-

[20] The following sections of U.S. Code were associated with the Sarbanes-Oxley Act: U.S. Code, Title 18, Crimes and Criminal Procedure, Part I, Crimes, Chapter 63, Mail Fraud and Other Fraud Offenses, Section 1348, Securities and Commodities Fraud, 1976; U.S. Code, Title 18, Crimes and Criminal Procedure, Part I, Crimes, Chapter 63, Mail Fraud and Other Fraud Offenses, Section 1349, Attempt and Conspiracy, 1976; U.S. Code, Title 18, Crimes and Criminal Procedure, Part I, Crimes, Chapter 63, Mail Fraud and Other Fraud Offenses, Section 1350, Failure of Corporate Officers to Certify Financial Reports, 1976; U.S. Code, Title 18, Crimes and Criminal Procedure, Part I, Crimes, Chapter 73, Obstruction of Justice, Section 1514A, Civil Action to Protect Against Retaliation in Fraud Cases, 1976; U.S. Code, Title 18, Crimes and Criminal Procedure, Part I, Crimes, Chapter 73, Obstruction of Justice, Section 1519, Destruction, Alteration, or Falsification of Records in Federal Investigations and Bankruptcy, 1976; U.S. Code, Title 18, Crimes and Criminal Procedure, Part I, Crimes, Chapter 73, Obstruction of Justice, Section 1520, Destruction of Corporate Audit Records, 1976.

ecutors are embracing this relatively new law to regulate corporate behavior.

Research has shown that FCPA prosecutions are also on the rise.[21] Gibson, Dunn and Crutcher attorneys identified an increase in FCPA enforcement by DOJ and the SEC.[22] From 2004 to 2011, there has been a steady increase in FCPA enforcement actions from both the SEC and DOJ, totaling 265 investigations and charges brought.[23] About nine times as many enforcement actions were initiated in 2011 than in 2004.[24]

The Garrett data appear to corroborate Gibson Dunn's findings that FCPA prosecutions are on the rise (see Figure 4.16). His database shows an increase in the number of defendants convicted in federal courts for violating the FCPA. The most dramatic increase was from 2009 to 2010, resulting in an increase of ten prosecutions.[25] Although this new increase in the use of the FCPA to police global corruption has raised concerns from the business community,[26] it is unlikely to stop anytime soon. Then–Assistant Attorney General Lanny A. Breuer

---

[21] Gibson, Dunn and Crutcher, *2011 Year End FCPA Update*, January 3, 2012; referenced September 10, 2012; Shearman and Sterling, *FCPA Digest: Cases and Review Releases Relating to Bribes to Foreign Officials Under the Foreign Corrupt Practices Act of 1977*, January 2012; referenced September 10, 2012. The number of FCPA enforcement actions found in this study is less than what Gibson Dunn reports. Nonetheless, Shearman and Sterling reports an increase in FCPA enforcement action in past several years.

[22] See Gibson Dunn, 2012, p. 2.

[23] See Gibson Dunn, 2012.

[24] See Gibson Dunn, 2012.

[25] Unfortunately, we could not supplement these analyses by using data from *Federal Court Cases: Integrated Data Base*. Indeed, we found no defendants convicted in federal courts under the U.S. Code responsible for the FCPA. When looking further, by searching dockets of FCPA cases, we found that prosecutors appear to bring charges under a federal law that prohibits conspiring to commit offenses against, or to defraud, the U.S. government (U.S. Code, Title 18, Crimes and Criminal Procedure, Part I, Crimes, Chapter 19, Conspiracy, Section 371, Conspiracy to Commit Offense or to Defraud United States, 1976). Because this conspiracy law can apply to a wide range of offenses or frauds that do not involve the FCPA, we cannot discern any trends pertaining to the FCPA from the *Federal Court Cases: Integrated Data Base* (Federal Judicial Center, 2011).

[26] Gibson Dunn, 2012, pp. 21–22.

**Figure 4.16**
**Federal Prosecutions for Foreign Corrupt Practices Act Offenses**

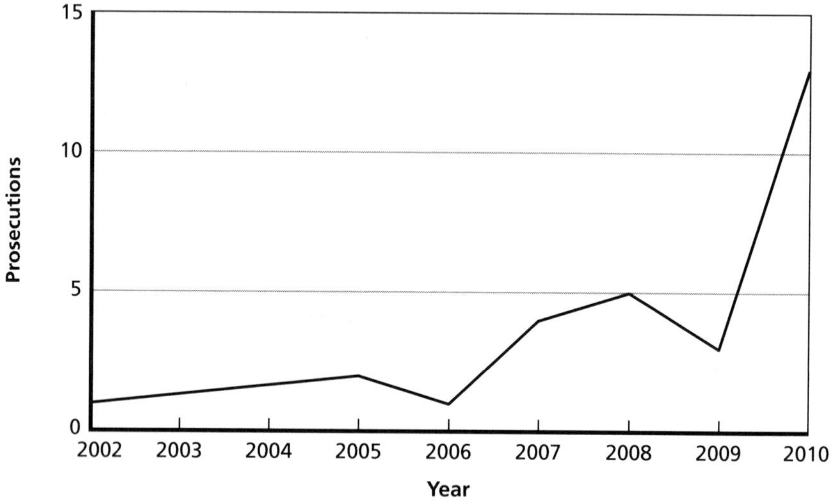


SOURCE: Garrett and Ashley, undated.
RAND *RR412-4.16*

stated at the American Conference Institute National Conference on the FCPA,

> [W]e have no intention whatsoever of supporting reforms whose aim is to weaken the FCPA and make it a less effective tool for fighting foreign bribery. . . . Having come this far, on what I believe is a noble journey, we cannot, and should not, start going backwards.[27]

This increase in FCPA prosecutions may be a partial explanation for the perception that some in the business community have of increased criminal prosecutorial activity.

---

[27] Lanny A. Breuer, assistant attorney general, remarks delivered at the 26th National Conference on the Foreign Corrupt Practices Act, Washington, D.C., November 8, 2011.

## Debarments

Government agencies use debarment and suspension to ensure that they contract with responsible companies. Debarred contractors are excluded from obtaining government contracts for a set period of time, depending on the law most applicable to the conduct.[28] Suspended contractors cannot obtain government contracts during an investigation or litigation pertaining to their conduct.[29]

Debarments and suspensions appear to be sharply increasing.[30] Table 4.1 illustrates the recent increase in debarment and suspension activity.

This recent increase, along with the increase in prosecutions under SOX and the FCPA, may also explain, in part, the perception of an increase in prosecutorial activity.

**Table 4.1**
**Recent Debarment and Suspension Activity**

| | Year | | |
|---|---|---|---|
| **Action** | **2009** | **2010** | **2011** |
| Suspensions | 417 | 612 | 928 |
| Parties proposed for debarment | 750 | 1,945 | 2,512 |
| Debarments | 1,501 | 1,651 | 2,398 |

SOURCE: Interagency Suspension and Debarment Committee (ISDC), 2011, 2012.

---

28 Kate M. Manuel, *Debarment and Suspension of Government Contractors: An Overview of the Law Including Recently Enacted and Proposed Amendments*, Washington, D.C.: Congressional Research Service, RL34753, January 6, 2012, p. 1.

29 Manuel, 2012.

30 Section 4 of Executive Order 12549 on debarment and suspension (Ronald Reagan, Debarment and Suspension, Executive Order 12549, February 18, 1986) directed the establishment of the ISDC to monitor implementation of the executive order, which, inter alia, requires all executive departments and agencies to participate in a government-wide system for debarment and suspension from programs and activities involving federal financial and nonfinancial assistance and benefits (Reagan, 1986). The committee issues regular reports that describe debarment activity and from which the data used in Table 4.1 were drawn.

## Summary

Overall, most types of prosecutions have *decreased* since the mid-1990s. This decline continued through the 2008 financial crisis and, at present, appears to have stabilized at a rate much lower than enforcement during the 1990s. But DPAs, NPAs, and debarments have increased in recent years, suggesting a greater reliance on what might be thought of as "noncriminal" approaches. More specifically, we found the following:

- The number of corporations convicted in federal courts has declined in the past decade.
- Large firms are more likely than smaller firms to be subject to prosecution.
- Individuals are usually prosecuted alongside corporations.
- Since 2003, use of DPAs and NPAs has increased.
- Prosecutions of corporate-related offenses, including investigations, have decreased in the past decade.
- Predominance in the use of civil law over criminal law, or vice versa, depends on the context.
- Enforcement of SOX and the FCPA have increased.

Debarment actions have dramatically increased. We see an increase in DPAs and NPAs following the prosecution of Arthur Andersen and the 2003 Holder memorandum. The increase in FCPA prosecutions corresponds with a recent emphasis placed by DOJ on curbing global corruption. These data also appear to corroborate reports on the lack of prosecutions related to the 2008 financial crisis.[31]

So how does the empirical evidence help us answer the question of whether there is an overcriminalization of corporate law? Ultimately, that question is not answerable without a normative theory of the correct level of criminalization. All we can offer is data on recent trends. On the one hand, the number of criminal prosecutions has declined in recent years for most types of cases, suggesting less prosecutorial activity, rather than more. On the other hand, use of DPAs and NPAs has

---

[31] See Peter J. Henning, "Dim Prospects for Financial Crisis Prosecutions," *New York Times DealBook*, May 29, 2012.

increased sharply, suggesting that the threat of criminal action is still playing an important role in governing corporate behavior. And debarment activity, in which government entities bar convicted corporations from doing business with them, has risen very sharply in the past three years.

CHAPTER FIVE

# Conclusions and Policy Implications

To consider the role of criminal law in the corporate context, we first described how the concept emerged. Originally, corporations were not criminally liable at all because of the intensely personal moral evaluation associated with criminal law and its general requirement of individual criminal intent. As restrictions on corporate criminal liability fell in the late 19th century, critics frequently decried the odd fit between the intentionality usually required in criminal law and corporate prosecutions. Yet despite this opposition, prosecutors, legislatures, and judges have long upheld these prosecutions, primarily on pragmatic grounds. Criminal penalties are justified, according to this view, not only because they are a useful incentive but also because criminal behavior that occurs within a corporation is otherwise very difficult to detect and prevent. With this justification, corporate criminal liability and criminal liability for corporate officers without requiring criminal intent has gradually expanded in the past 150 years. This pragmatic justification for criminal liability has important implications that we discuss in this chapter.

We next turned to developments in this area in the past 30 years. The Federal Sentencing Guidelines began a shift toward reforming corporations from within by developing compliance programs and structural reform. At first, this occurred as a condition of probation after a corporation was convicted, but gradually the incentives to having a robust compliance program have increased and are often relevant to the decision as to whether to prosecute a case in the first place. The downfall of Arthur Andersen as the result of a conviction on a legal theory that was subsequently rejected by the U.S. Supreme Court highlighted the risks of going to trial for corporate directors and of unintended collateral consequences for prosecutors. DPAs and NPAs boomed in its aftermath but have created their own complications.

Finally, we examined the available data to identify trends in the use of the criminal law in this context. We found that, in general, formal prosecutions are declining in number across a broad range of areas. Two important exceptions, however, are prosecutions under SOX and the FCPA, which have both become more common. We also noted a huge growth in the number of DPAs and NPAs and the substantial recent increase in debarment proceedings.

Our analysis suggests that we may have reached an odd juncture in the history of the use of criminal penalties in the corporate context. Corporations and their directors are hesitant to directly challenge prosecutorial theories for fear of the collateral consequences. The federal government is independently increasing debarment and suspension proceedings in an effort to minimize waste and fraud. The result is the huge increase in NPAs and DPAs, which lack many of the key benefits of public law. Given that so many investigations are settled even before the formal filing of criminal charges, there is little or no judicial oversight over prosecutorial decisionmaking and case resolution, no formal fact-finding, and no development of the law. With little oversight, corporations may sometimes face pressure to effectively investigate and develop cases against individual wrongdoers. The result has been a kind of privatization of corporate criminal law.

## What Lessons Can We Draw for Policymakers?

Whatever the ultimate merits of the institution of corporate criminal liability, the genie is long out of the bottle, and arguments about abolishing the institution of corporate criminal liability are likely of interest only to theorists. Still, policymakers should be cautious about the use of criminal law in this context. Although it may be understandably tempting to criminally punish corporations that wield great power, legislators and prosecutors should recognize the complications inherent in applying the criminal law to a legal fiction. The temptation to punish a "bad" corporation can lead to harming thousands of innocent stakeholders who were completely blameless. Although the pursuit of corporate criminal liability may be a useful tool to discover and deter criminal activity *by individuals* within organizations, the kind of moral condemnation that is usually associated with a criminal penalty is not typically useful in thinking about the culpability of a large entity. Anthropomorphic thinking—attributing individual moral states to an organization—can obscure the true culpability (or lack thereof) of individuals.

Individual criminal liability absent criminal intent poses its own complications. Although the urge to use the criminal law to hold someone responsible for the consequences of his or her actions is understandable, we should remember that the requirement of criminal intent has been central to our collective understanding of criminal sanctions. Exceptions to the general rule that the criminal law requires criminal intentionality should remain exceptions. Although criminal intent is not an absolute prerequisite to criminal liability, it is no coincidence that it has remained a central part of Anglo-American criminal law. Exceptions to this general rule should remain narrowly tailored to address specific dangers.

### Recognize That Criminal Sanctions Are Instrumental Tools and Not Moral Judgments

Although, as many have long argued, criminal liability may be a useful tool in the organizational context, we must recognize it as just that—an instrumental tool. The theory that an offending organization *deserves* punishment in a retributive sense makes very little sense. The entity Arthur Andersen was prosecuted, but thousands of individual people were effectively punished. It is difficult to construct any kind of principled argument that they deserved to be so. Instead, they should be recognized as collateral damage in an effort to provide incentives for corporations to self-police and identify individual wrongdoers.[1]

---

[1] This kind of collateral damage is not unprecedented—the criminal law inflicts this quite regularly whenever the law imprisons a parent, partner, or caretaker. But at least in the indi-

Similarly, we should recognize that a prosecution of an individual for actions or inactions of others is generally not a moral condemnation of that individual and should not be understood as such.[2]

The fact that criminal law in this context is primarily justified by its instrumental functionality has important implications. If criminal law is used and justified as an instrumental tool in this context, we should carefully weigh the costs and benefits of its use. This kind of cost–benefit analysis is often not done in the criminal law context because of the noninstrumental function of criminal law. We morally condemn and prosecute murderers because murder is wrong—not primarily because it is efficient to do so. But if we are using criminal law principally to create corporate governance incentives, we should think carefully about whether the benefits outweigh the costs. The instinct to punish "bad" corporations can prevent us from conducting this analysis.

Similarly, we should carefully scrutinize the temptation to punish individuals associated with a bad event absent proof of criminal intent. Although it may be tempting to want to find someone to punish in the wake of a bad event, such punishment also may not be the most effective way to ensure compliance.

Although the benefits of using criminal penalties to provide instrumental incentives are obvious, the costs may be less so. The collateral consequences of prosecuting a corporation criminally can be vast and hard to predict. Criminally punishing individuals who are guilty of poor judgment or bad luck or for the actions of their employees may create incentives, but only at the cost of diluting the collective significance of the criminal sanction.

---

vidual context, the individual moral condemnation associated with the criminal law is more understandable and reflects our collective judgment better than the incidental punishment of stakeholders.

[2] Conventional criminal law also contains doctrines that sometimes apply criminal penalties to those without criminal intent. For example, the felony-murder doctrine makes an accomplice in a felony guilty of murder if someone is killed during the commission of the felony, even if the accomplice did not intend for anyone to die during commission of the crime. Such doctrines are often criticized for many of the same reasons laid out here.

What circumstances might justify the use of criminal sanctions in the corporate context? Here, we might learn from conspiracy law. Neal Kumar Katyal has argued that the unique organizational dangers of criminal conspiracies justify elements of conspiracy law that have often been criticized (including aspects of strict liability).[3] Policymakers interested in controlling corporate malfeasance should reserve the use of criminal law to target the particular dangers of illegal activity within larger organizations. More specifically, the enormous advantages of specialization can make criminal activity within organizations much more dangerous than that of an individual operating alone. The power of an individual criminal is much more limited than that of one operating in conjunction with others. Similarly, the unique social psychological effects of groups can make it more difficult for an individual to resist social pressure within an organization. Exceptions to the general rule of individual criminal liability should be carefully tailored to such dangers.

Prosecutors must also recognize the complications in this area. This includes recognizing that the enormous leverage they possess can create incentives for corporations and outsourced investigations to identify scapegoats. They must also recognize the risk of collateral damage to innocent parties. Although this is always a risk in criminal law—defendants often have innocent families who are deeply damaged by the state's action—the diffusion of harm to innocent parties in this context can be different.

### Have Judges Review Deferred and Nonprosecution Agreements

Partly as a result of recognizing the limitations of the formal use of criminal law, use of DPAs and NPAs has skyrocketed. These agreements avoid some of the harms associated with using the criminal law that we have described. But many of the very things that make these agreements attractive to both corporations and prosecutors raise their own problems. The lack of judicial oversight over the agreements have led to concerns about their scope, conflicts of interest, and the institu-

---

[3] Neal Kumar Katyal, "Conspiracy Theory," *Yale Law Journal*, Vol. 112, June 2003, pp. 1307–1398.

tional competence of prosecutors to mandate potentially far-reaching changes in business practices. These problems are best remedied by judicial oversight. Just as a plea agreement has to be reviewed by the relevant judge, so should NPAs and DPAs. This would provide some assurance that the agreements are genuinely in the public good and might allow third parties who are affected by the agreements (e.g., individual defendants) to have objections heard in a neutral forum. Such review should include the factual basis of the agreement, fairness to third parties, genuine independence of the monitor, and nexus of the terms of the agreement and the alleged wrongdoing. Policymakers should give serious consideration to requiring that DPAs and NPAs be reviewed by an appropriate federal judge. This would provide additional oversight and transparency and reassure the public that justice was being served.

### Carefully Review Debarment Provisions

The interaction of the enormous growth in the criminal law with debarment provisions can also lead to unintended consequences. Debarment proceedings are typically initiated by agencies that do not want to do business with organizations convicted of crimes. Yet debarment provisions have led to rational corporations being unwilling to take even strong cases to trial for fear that the viability of the company itself may be at stake.

As a result, the de facto law becomes what the most aggressive prosecutor in the most aggressive jurisdiction says it is. This sidesteps judicial oversight and the public quality of criminal law. The lack of litigation also halts the development of the common law. Rather than being provided guidance through a series of appellate decisions from neutral Article III judges with lifetime tenure, stakeholders are left only with guidance from prosecutors who are beholden to the more-political, elected executive branches.

Debarment provisions that automatically require a licensing agency or an entity of government to refuse to do business or refuse to license a corporation upon the corporations' indictment or conviction should be carefully reviewed by policymakers. Rather than a *per se* rule that requires this potentially catastrophic outcome for the corporation, the relevant governmental agency should make the decision on a case-by-case basis, subject to appeal to the federal courts, depending on the severity of the allegations made and their relevance to the domain of the governmental entity.

### Substitute the Use of Civil Sanctions

Can civil sanctions serve as an important substitute? Historically, civil penalties have lacked the formal expressive function of the criminal law.[4] As the most serious formal sanction that a jurisdiction can impose, criminal convictions represented a particular collective moral judgment about the wrongness of an act that a civil sanction lacked. Yet, as noted above, this kind of collective moral judgment fits oddly with the legal fiction of a corporation.[5]

And with the rise of NPAs and DPAs, some of these characteristics of a criminal sanction have disappeared. NPAs and DPAs often do not require a formal admission of guilt or, in some cases, any public acknowledgment of wrongdoing. They completely avoid the public expressive rituals of the courthouse and the oversight of a federal judge. In these ways, NPAs and DPAs lack some of the conventional benefits of a public criminal sanction.

There may, therefore, be a role for a civil sanction that includes explicit fact-finding and a finding of culpability on the part of the organization. Historically, the SEC has settled civil fraud charges while allowing a company to neither admit nor deny the charges.[6] However,

---

[4] Khanna, 1996, p. 1497 (noting that the unique sanctioning characteristic of criminal law is its stigmatizing effect). This was particularly true when the SEC routinely permitted corporations to settle civil fraud charges while neither admitting nor denying charges.

[5] Khanna has noted that corporate criminal sanctions may have developed because, when they developed, the modern administrative state necessary to use civil sanctions had not been developed. In other words, our reliance on criminal rather than civil sanctions is, in part, an accident of history (Khanna, 1996, p. 1486: "Given the absence of widespread public civil enforcement prior to the early 1900s, corporate criminal liability appears to have been the only available option that met both the need for public enforcement and the need for corporate liability").

[6] Senator Elizabeth Warren has recently questioned the SEC's practice of settling civil fraud charges without admitting or denying the charges (Andrew Ackerman, "Sen. Warren Targets Wall Street Settlements," *Wall Street Journal Washington Wire*, May 14, 2013; see

the new chair of the SEC, Mary Jo White, has recently announced that, at least in some cases, the SEC will require the corporation to admit wrongdoing.[7] This may increase the ability of civil fines to fulfill the expressive function of law by combining formal fact-finding and an admission of wrongdoing—two elements that are absent from criminal allegations resolved with NPAs and DPAs.[8]

Ideally, such a sanction would sidestep the hard-to-predict collateral consequences that are associated with criminal sanctions. Similarly, by categorizing the sanction as civil, we might avoid some of the long-noted odd disjunctures between the religious origins of the criminal law's focus on individual culpability and the legal fiction of a corporation, including the temptation to anthropomorphize the corporation. And it might serve as a more attractive intermediate sanction—a way of providing regulators a smoother continuum of possible punishments between the severity of criminal penalties or the tap on the wrist of a nominal fine paid without any admission of wrongdoing. Criminal sanctions should still be retained for cases of individual wrongdoing where there is the appropriate *mens rea*.

The rationale for the applicability of the criminal law in this area has long been pragmatic—that it was necessary to identify wrongdoing cloaked in the opacity of an organization. Yet it is unclear why criminal sanctions are uniquely suited to that role. Civil sanctions of significant magnitude and severity might serve that function just as well as, if not better than, criminal sanctions. Structural reform and compliance programs could be motivated by enhanced civil rather than criminal sanctions. And by not having quite the collateral consequences associated with criminal penalties, civil sanctions are more likely to face appropriate challenge by companies and their directors. This would advance

also Samuel L. Buell, "Potentially Perverse Effects of Corporate Criminal Liability," in Anthony S. Barkow and Rachel E. Barkow, eds., *Prosecutors in the Boardroom: Using Criminal Law to Regulate Corporate Conduct*, New York: New York University Press, 2011, pp. 87–109, arguing generally for increased use of civil sanctions).

7 However, most will still be resolved on the conventional terms (James B. Stewart, "S.E.C. Has a Message for Firms Not Used to Admitting Guilt," *New York Times*, June 21, 2013).

8 On the other hand, it is important to acknowledge the limitations of the SEC, which has jurisdiction only over publicly traded companies listed on U.S. exchanges.

the development of the common law and further the public benefits of litigation in clarifying the law.

In some ways, our current system of nominally criminal enforcement already resembles a civil system (albeit one with a very powerful regulatory authority). Formal criminal proceedings are very rare, almost no one is incarcerated, and the most common outcome is some kind of company-funded enhanced compliance program—a de facto fine. The heightened standard of proof that typically distinguishes criminal from civil cases is all but irrelevant because cases are settled early—not in the shadow of criminal trial, but in the shadow of the collateral consequences of indictment.

So what difference does it make whether we label the regime criminal or civil? More than 20 years ago, Yale Law School Dean Abraham S. Goldstein noted the complexity of applying the right set of procedures, particularly with civil and criminal concepts mixed:

> The challenge now is to . . . recognize that each civil and criminal remedy is part of a network of sanctions designed to control deviant behavior, to provide screening mechanisms to determine which sanction should be brought to bear, and by whom, in order to make law enforcement more effective overall; and to create the hybrid procedures uniquely appropriate to each of these hybrid processes. If we do not succeed in meeting this challenge, there is a genuine risk that the stigma and sanctions associated with "crime" will be imposed, in both civil and criminal processes, on persons who are not culpable in any widely accepted sense of that term. If that happens, if offenders who do not match the public image of criminality are too casually found to be criminal, the "crime" label will lose its incremental utility, the moral force of the criminal sanction will be dissipated, and many more people will suffer unjust treatment.[9]

Goldstein's fears remain germane. A complex web of laws and regulations creates incentives for corporate and individual behavior that is

---

[9] Abraham S. Goldstein, "White-Collar Crime and Civil Sanctions," *Yale Law Journal*, Vol. 101, No. 8, June 1992, pp. 1895–1899.

in the public interest. Adjusting one strand in the web, even for the best of reasons, can lead to unanticipated consequences. It seems unlikely, for example, that the prosecutors involved in the Andersen cases anticipated that their actions would lead to the rise of NPAs and DPAs and the reduced transparency that has resulted. To improve behavior in and by organizations, we may have relied too heavily on sanctions labeled "criminal" in recent years. This has led to corporations and directors being reluctant to litigate, at a cost of the development of the common law and public transparency. By relying more on civil sanctions, the U.S. justice system might be better harmonized in this unique context. A more cautious approach to the use of criminal sanctions would preserve the expressive power that criminal sanctions should possess.

# References


Abrams, Norman, "Criminal Liability of Corporate Officers for Strict Liability Offenses—A Comment on *Dotterweich* and *Park*," *UCLA Law Review*, Vol. 28, No. 3, February 1981, pp. 463–477.

Ackerman, Andrew, "Sen. Warren Targets Wall Street Settlements," *Wall Street Journal Washington Wire*, May 14, 2013. As of September 18, 2014: http://blogs.wsj.com/washwire/2013/05/14/sen-warren-targets-wall-street-settlements/

Alexander, Cindy R., Jennifer Arlen, and Mark A. Cohen, "Regulating Corporate Criminal Sanctions: Federal Guidelines and the Sentencing of Public Firms," *Journal of Law and Economics*, Vol. 42, No. S1, April 1999, pp. 393–422.

Alexander, Delroy, Greg Burns, Robert Manor, Flynn McRoberts, and E. A. Torriero, "The Fall of Andersen," *Hartford Courant*, November 1, 2002.

Alschuler, Albert, "Ancient Law and the Punishment of Corporations: Of Frankpledge and Deodand," *Boston University Law Review*, Vol. 71, 1991, pp. 307–313.

American Law Institute, *Model Penal Code: Tentative Draft No. 4*, Philadelphia, Pa., 1955.

———, *Model Penal Code: Proposed Official Draft*, Philadelphia, Pa., 1962.

Anderson, James M., and Paul Heaton, "How Much Difference Does the Lawyer Make? The Effect of Defense Counsel on Murder Case Outcomes," *Yale Law Journal*, Vol. 122, No. 1, October 2012, pp. 154–172.

Anderson, James M., Jeffrey R. Kling, and Kate Stith, "Measuring Interjudge Sentencing Disparity: Before and After the Federal Sentencing Guidelines," *Journal of Law and Economics*, Vol. 42, No. S1, April 1999, pp. 271–308.

Anonymous, 88 Eng. Rep. 1518, K.B. 1701.

Arlen, Jennifer, "Removing Prosecutors from the Boardroom: Limiting Prosecutorial Discretion to Impose Structural Reforms," in Anthony S. Barkow and Rachel E. Barkow, eds., *Prosecutors in the Boardroom: Using Criminal Law to Regulate Corporate Conduct*, New York: New York University Press, 2011, pp. 62–86.

*Arthur Andersen LLP v. United States*, 544 U.S. 696, 125 S. Ct. 2129 (2005).

Bacon, Francis, *The Elements of the Common Lawes of England: Branched into a Double Trial*, Clark, N.J.: Lawbook Exchange Ltd., 2003.

Barkow, Anthony S., and Rachel E. Barkow, "Introduction," in Anthony S. Barkow and Rachel E. Barkow, eds., *Prosecutors in the Boardroom: Using Criminal Law to Regulate Corporate Conduct*, New York: New York University Press, 2011, pp. 1–10.

*Barnes v. State*, 19 Conn. 398 (1849).

Bishop, Joel Prentiss, *Commentaries on the Criminal Law*, 3rd ed., Boston, Mass.: Little, Brown, 1865.

BJS—*See* U.S. Department of Justice, Office of Justice Programs, Bureau of Justice Statistics.

Blackstone, William, *Commentaries on the Laws of England*, Oxford: Clarendon Press, 1765.

*Boson v. Sandford*, 90 Eng. Rep. 377 (K.B. 1690).

Bowman, Frank O., III, "A Challenge to the Rationale for General Economic Crime Sentence Increases Following Sarbanes-Oxley: Letter of Frank Bowman to U.S. Sentencing Commission," *Federal Sentencing Reporter*, Vol. 15, No. 4, April 2003a, pp. 284–290.

———, "Editor's Observations: The Sarbanes-Oxley Act and What Came After," *Federal Sentencing Reporter*, Vol. 15, No. 4, April 2003b, pp. 231–233.

Bracton, Henry de, *On the Laws and Customs of England*, George E. Woodbine, ed., Samuel E. Thorne, trans., Cambridge: Belknap Press of Harvard University Press, 1968.

Breuer, Lanny A., assistant attorney general, remarks delivered at the 26th National Conference on the Foreign Corrupt Practices Act, Washington, D.C., November 8, 2011. As of September 30, 2014:
http://www.justice.gov/criminal/pr/speeches/2011/crm-speech-111108.html

Breyer, Stephen, "The Federal Sentencing Guidelines and the Key Compromises Upon Which They Rest," *Hofstra Law Review*, Vol. 17, No. 1, Fall 1988, pp. 1–50.

Brickey, Kathleen F., "Corporate Criminal Accountability: A Brief History and an Observation," *Washington University Law Quarterly*, Vol. 60, No. 2, 1982a, pp. 393–423.

———, "Criminal Liability of Corporate Officers for Strict Liability Offenses—Another View," *Vanderbilt Law Review*, Vol. 35, No. 6, November 1982b, pp. 1337–1382.

Buell, Samuel L., "The Blaming Function of Entity Criminal Liability," *Indiana Law Journal*, Vol. 81, 2006, pp. 473–537.

———, "Potentially Perverse Effects of Corporate Criminal Liability," in Anthony S. Barkow and Rachel E. Barkow, eds., *Prosecutors in the Boardroom: Using Criminal Law to Regulate Corporate Conduct*, New York: New York University Press, 2011, pp. 87–109.

———, "Is the White Collar Offender Privileged?" *Duke Law Journal*, Vol. 63, No. 4, January 2014, pp. 823–889.

*Carroll v. State*, 63 Md. 551, 3 A. 29 (1885).

*Case of Sutton's Hospital*, 77 Eng. Rep. 960 (K.B. 1612).

*Chuter v. Freeth & Pocock Ltd.*, 2 K.B. 832 (1911).

Coffee, John C., Jr., "'No Soul to Damn: No Body to Kick': An Unscandalized Inquiry into the Problem of Corporate Punishment," *Michigan Law Review*, Vol. 79, No. 3, January 1981, pp. 386–459.

Cohen, Mark A., "Corporate Crime and Punishment: An Update on Sentencing Practice in the Federal Courts, 1988–1990," *Boston University Law Review*, Vol. 71, No. 2, March 1991, pp. 247–280.

Coke, Sir Edward, *The Third Part of the Institutes of the Laws of England: Concerning High Treason, and Other Pleas of the Crown, and Criminall Causes*, London: M. Flesher, 1641.

*Commonwealth v. Farren*, 91 Mass. 489 (1864).

*Commonwealth v. Hancock Free Bridge Corp.*, 68 Mass. 58 (1854).

*Commonwealth v. Proprietors of New Bedford Bridge*, 68 Mass. 339 (1854).

*Commonwealth v. Pulaski County Agricultural & Mechanical Ass'n*, 92 Ky. 197, 17 S.W. 442 (1891).

Connaughton, Jeff, *The Payoff: Why Wall Street Always Wins*, Westport, Conn.: Prospecta Press, 2012.

Corporate Crime Reporter, *Crime Without Conviction: The Rise of Deferred and Non Prosecution Agreements*, Washington, D.C., December 28, 2005. As of September 18, 2014:
http://www.corporatecrimereporter.com/deferredreport.htm

Cuomo, Anthony A., "*Mens Rea* and Status Criminality," *Southern California Law Review*, Vol. 40, No. 3, Spring 1967, pp. 463–528.

Denno, Deborah W., "Criminal Law in a Post-Freudian World," *University of Illinois Law Review*, Vol. 2005, 2005, pp. 601–774.

Douglass, David L., and Winifred M. Weitsen, "Overcriminalization of Corporate Acts: What Is a General Counsel to Do?" *In-House Defense Quarterly*, Winter 2013, pp. 26–31.

Doyle, James M., "Learning from Error in American Criminal Justice," *Journal of Criminal Law and Criminology*, Vol. 100, No. 1, Winter 2010, pp. 109–148.

Eichenwald, Kurt, "Andersen Refused a Probation Deal," *New York Times*, April 2, 2002. As of September 18, 2014:
http://www.nytimes.com/2002/04/02/business/andersen-refused-a-probation-deal.html

Elkins, James R., "Corporations and the Criminal Law: An Uneasy Alliance," *Kentucky Law Journal*, Vol. 65, No. 1, 1976, pp. 73–129.

EOUSA—*See* Executive Office for U.S. Attorneys.

Epstein, Richard A., "Contingent Commissions in Insurance: A Legal and Economic Analysis," *Competition Policy International*, Vol. 3, 2007, p. 281.

Executive Office for U.S. Attorneys, *United States Attorneys' Manual*, Washington, D.C.: U.S. Department of Justice, 1997. As of November 7, 2014:
http://purl.access.gpo.gov/GPO/LPS1220

Federal Judicial Center, *Federal Court Cases: Integrated Data Base*, Ann Arbor, Mich.: Inter-university Consortium for Political and Social Research, 2011. As of October 21, 2014:
http://doi.org/10.3886/ICPSR33622.v2

Filip, Mark, deputy attorney general, "Principles of Federal Prosecution of Business Organizations," memorandum to heads of department components and U.S. Attorneys, August 28, 2008.

Fiss, Owen M., "Against Settlement," *Yale Law Journal*, Vol. 93, No. 6, May 1984, pp. 1073–1090.

Fisse, W. B., "The Social Policy of Corporate Criminal Responsibility," *Adelaide Law Review*, Vol. 6, No. 3, 1977–1978, pp. 361–412.

Friedman, Howard M., "Some Reflections on the Corporation as Criminal Defendant," *Notre Dame Law Review*, Vol. 55, No. 2, December 1, 1979, pp. 173–202.

Gallo, Joseph C., Kenneth Dau-Schmidt, Joseph L. Craycraft, and Charles J. Parker, "Department of Justice Antitrust Enforcement, 1995–1997: An Empirical Study," *Review of Industrial Organization*, Vol. 17, 2000, pp. 75–133.

*Gardner v. Broderick*, 392 U.S. 273 (1968).

Garrett, Brandon L., "Structural Reform Prosecution," *Virginia Law Review*, Vol. 93, No. 4, June 2007, pp. 853–957.

———, "Globalized Corporate Prosecutions," *Virginia Law Review*, Vol. 97, No. 8, December 2011, pp. 1775–1876.

Garrett, Brandon L., and Jon Ashley, "Federal Organizational Plea Agreements," Charlottesville, Va.: University of Virginia School of Law, undated. As of October 22, 2014:
http://lib.law.virginia.edu/Garrett/plea_agreements/home.php

———, "Federal Organizational Prosecution Agreements," last updated October 27, 2014. As of October 27, 2014:
http://lib.law.virginia.edu/Garrett/prosecution_agreements/home.suphp

Gibbon, Edward, *The Decline and Fall of the Roman Empire*, Vol. 2: *Chapters XVI–XXV*, New York: Alfred A. Knopf, 1993.

Gibson Dunn—*See* Gibson, Dunn and Crutcher.

Gibson, Dunn and Crutcher, *2011 Year End FCPA Update*, January 3, 2012; referenced September 10, 2012. As of September 20, 2014:
http://www.gibsondunn.com/publications/Pages/2011YearEndFCPAUpdate.aspx

"Going Soft on Corporate Crime," *New York Times*, editorial, April 10, 2008. As of September 20, 2014:
http://www.nytimes.com/2008/04/10/opinion/10thu2.html?_r=0

Goldstein, Abraham S., "White-Collar Crime and Civil Sanctions," *Yale Law Journal*, Vol. 101, No. 8, June 1992, pp. 1895–1899.

*Graham v. Allis-Chalmers Mfg. Co.*, 188 A.2d 125, 41 Del. Ch. 78, January 24, 1963.

Griffin, Lisa Kern, "Inside-Out Enforcement," in Anthony S. Barkow and Rachel E. Barkow, eds., *Prosecutors in the Boardroom: Using Criminal Law to Regulate Corporate Conduct*, New York: New York University Press, 2011, pp. 110–131.

Hall, Jerome, *General Principles of Criminal Law*, Indianapolis, Ind.: Bobbs-Merrill Company, 1947.

Henning, Peter J., "Dim Prospects for Financial Crisis Prosecutions," *New York Times DealBook*, May 29, 2012. As of September 20, 2014:
http://dealbook.nytimes.com/2012/05/29/dim-prospects-for-financial-crisis-prosecutions/

Heritage Foundation, "Overcriminalization," *Solutions 2014*, undated; referenced February 28, 2014. As of October 22, 2014:
http://solutions.heritage.org/overcriminalization/

Hippard, James J., Sr., "The Unconstitutionality of Criminal Liability Without Fault: An Argument for a Constitutional Doctrine of Mens Rea," *Houston Law Review*, Vol. 10, No. 5, July 1973, pp. 1039–1058.

Holder, Eric, deputy attorney general, "Bringing Criminal Charges Against Corporations," memorandum to all component heads and U.S. Attorneys, Washington, D.C., June 16, 1999. As of September 20, 2014: http://www.justice.gov/criminal/fraud/documents/reports/1999/charging-corps.PDF

Holland, Lady Saba Holland, *Memoir of the Reverend Sydney Smith*, Sarah Austin, ed., New York: Harper and Bros., 1855.

Holmes, Oliver Wendell, Jr., *The Common Law*, Boston, Mass.: Little, Brown, and Company, 1881.

Ide, R. William, III, *ABA Presidential Task Force on the Attorney–Client Privilege*, August 2006.

Interagency Suspension and Debarment Committee, *Report by the Interagency Suspension and Debarment Committee on Federal Agency Suspension and Disbarment Activities*, c. 2011. As of September 30, 2014: https://isdc.sites.usa.gov/files/2014/02/isdc_section_873_report1.pdf

———, *Report by the Interagency Suspension and Debarment Committee on Federal Agency Suspension and Disbarment Activities*, c. 2012. As of September 30, 2014: https://isdc.sites.usa.gov/files/2014/02/isdc_section_873_fy_2011_report_to_congress_lieberman.pdf

Kadish, Sanford H., "Some Observations on the Use of Criminal Sanctions in Enforcing Economic Regulations," *University of Chicago Law Review*, Vol. 30, No. 3, Spring 1963, pp. 423–449.

Katyal, Neal Kumar, "Conspiracy Theory," *Yale Law Journal*, Vol. 112, June 2003, p. 1307–1398.

Khanna, V. S., "Corporate Criminal Liability: What Purpose Does It Serve?" *Harvard Law Review*, Vol. 109, No. 7, May 1996, pp. 1477–1534.

Kher, Unmesh, "The End of Arthur Andersen?" *Time*, March 11, 2002. As of September 21, 2014: http://content.time.com/time/business/article/0,8599,216386,00.html

Levin, Marc A., "At the State Level, So-Called Crimes Are Here, There, Everywhere," *Criminal Justice*, Vol. 28, No. 1, Spring 2013, pp. 4–9.

Lindley, Nathaniel, "On the Principles Which Govern the Criminal and Civil Responsibilities of Corporations (March 30, 1857)," in *Juridical Society Papers*, Vol. 2, March 30, 1857, pp. 34–35.

Manuel, Kate M., *Debarment and Suspension of Government Contractors: An Overview of the Law Including Recently Enacted and Proposed Amendments*, Washington, D.C.: Congressional Research Service, RL34753, January 6, 2012.

McNulty, Paul J., deputy attorney general, "Principles of Federal Prosecution of Business Organizations," memorandum to heads of department components and U.S. Attorneys, December 2006.

*Milbrath v. State*, 138 Wis. 354, 120 N.W. 252 (1909).

Miller, Samuel R., "Corporate Criminal Liability: A Principle Extended to Its Limits," *Federal Bar Journal*, Vol. 38, No. 1, 1979, pp. 49–68.

Morford, Craig S., acting deputy attorney general, "Selection and Use of Monitors in Deferred Prosecution Agreements and Non-Prosecution Agreements with Corporations," memorandum to heads of department components and U.S. Attorneys, March 7, 2008. As of September 20, 2014:
http://www.justice.gov/sites/default/files/dag/legacy/2008/03/20/morford-useofmonitorsmemo-03072008.pdf

*Morissette v. United States*, 342 U.S. 246, 72 S. Ct. 240 (1952).

Mueller, Gerhard O. W., "*Mens Rea* and the Corporation: A Study of the Model Penal Code Position on Corporate Criminal Liability," *University of Pittsburgh Law Review*, Vol. 19, No. 1, Fall 1957, pp. 21–50.

———, "On Common Law Mens Rea," *Minnesota Law Review*, Vol. 42, No. 6, May 1958, pp. 1043–1104.

*New York Central R. Co. v. United States*, 212 U.S. 481 (1909).

Occupy Wall Street, "About," undated; referenced June 3, 2013. As of September 20, 2014:
http://occupywallst.org/about/

Odato, James M., "NYRA Deal in the Works," *Albany Times Union*, December 6, 2003, p. A1.

*People v. Corporation*, 11 Wend. 539, N.Y. Sup. Ct. (1834).

*People v. Detroit Lead Works*, 82 Mich. 471, 46 N.W. 735 (1890).

*People v. John H. Woodbury Dermatological Institute*, 192 N.Y. 454 (1908).

*People v. Roby*, 52 Mich. 577, 18 N.W. 365 (1884).

*People ex rel. Price v. Sheffield Farms-Slawson-Decker Co.*, 225 N.Y. 25, 121 N.E. 474 (Ct. App. N.Y. 1918).

Pillsbury, Samuel H., "Evil and the Law of Murder," *University of California Davis Law Review*, Vol. 24, No. 2, Winter 1990, pp. 437–488.

Pollock, Frederick, "Has the Common Law Received the Fiction Theory of Corporations?" *Law Quarterly Review*, Vol. 27, No. 2, 1911, pp. 219–235.

Pollock, Frederick, and Frederic William Maitland, *The History of English Law Before the Time of Edward I*, 2nd ed., London: Cambridge University Press, 1968.

Posner, Richard A., "A Statistical Study of Antitrust Enforcement," *Journal of Law and Economics*, Vol. 13, No. 2, October 1970, pp. 365–419.

Poynder, John, *Literary Extracts from English and Other Works: Collected During Half a Century Together with Some Original Matter*, London: J. Hatchard and Son, 1844.

Public Law 75-718, Fair Labor Standards Act of 1938, June 25, 1938.

Public Law 80-806, Commodity Credit Corporation Charter Act of 1948, June 29, 1948.

Public Law 89-487, amending § 3 of the Administrative Procedure Act, July 4, 1966. As of September 25, 2014:
http://www.gpo.gov/fdsys/pkg/STATUTE-80/pdf/STATUTE-80-Pg250.pdf

Public Law 95-213, Foreign Corrupt Practices Act, December 19, 1977.

Public Law 98-473, joint resolution for continuing appropriations, October 12, 1984. As of September 25, 2014:
http://www.gpo.gov/fdsys/pkg/STATUTE-98/pdf/STATUTE-98-Pg1837.pdf

Public Law 107-204, Sarbanes-Oxley Act of 2002, July 30, 2002. As of September 25, 2014:
http://www.gpo.gov/fdsys/pkg/PLAW-107publ204/content-detail.html

Public Law 111-203, Dodd-Frank Wall Street Reform and Consumer Protection Act, July 21, 2010.

Reagan, Ronald, Debarment and Suspension, Executive Order 12549, February 18, 1986.

*Regina v. Great North of England R. Co.*, 9 Q.B. 315, 115 Eng. Rep. 1294 (1846).

Reichert, Alan K., Michael Lockett, and Ramesh P. Rao, "The Impact of Illegal Business Practice on Shareholder Returns," *Financial Review*, Vol. 31, No. 1, February 1996, pp. 67–85.

*Rex v. Huggins*, 93 Eng. Rep. 915 (K.B. 1730).

*Rex v. Medley*, 6 Car. & P. 292, 172 Eng. Rep. 1246 (K.B. 1834).

"Saxbe to Get Tough with Price-Fixers," *Antitrust and Trade Regulation Report*, No. 683, October 8, 1974, p. A-5.

Sayre, Francis Bowes, "Mens Rea," *Harvard Law Review*, Vol. 45, 1932, p. 974.

———, "Public Welfare Offenses," *Columbia Law Review*, Vol. 33, 1933, pp. 55–56.

Shearman and Sterling, *FCPA Digest: Cases and Review Releases Relating to Bribes to Foreign Officials Under the Foreign Corrupt Practices Act of 1977*, January 2012; referenced September 10, 2012. As of September 20, 2014: http://www.shearman.com/files/Publication/bb1a7bff-ad52-4cf9-88b9-9d99e001dd5f/Presentation/PublicationAttachment/590a9fc7-2617-41fc-9aef-04727f927e07/FCPA-Digest-Jan2012.pdf

Shepherd, William, "A Country Overburdened by Too Many Laws," *Criminal Justice*, Vol. 28, No. 1, Spring 2013.

Silver-Greenberg, Jessica, "E-Mails Imply JPMorgan Knew Some Mortgage Deals Were Bad," *New York Times DealBook*, February 6, 2013, p. B1. As of September 20, 2014: http://dealbook.nytimes.com/2013/02/06/e-mails-imply-jpmorgan-knew-some-mortgage-deals-were-bad/

Skantz, Terrance R., Dale O. Cloniger, and Thomas H. Strickland, "Price-Fixing and Shareholder Returns: An Empirical Study," *Financial Review*, Vol. 25, No. 1, February 1990, pp. 153–163.

*Southern Express Co. v. State*, 1 Ga. App. 700, 58 S.E. 67 (1907).

Spivack, Peter, and Sujit Raman, "Regulating the 'New Regulators': Current Trends in Deferred Prosecution Agreements," *American Criminal Law Review*, Vol. 45, 2008, pp. 159–167.

*Staples v. United States*, 511 U.S. 600, 114 S. Ct. 1793 (1994).

*State v. B. & O. R. R. Co.*, 15 W.Va. 362 (1879).

*State v. Burnam*, 71 Wash. 199, 128 P. 218 (1912).

*State v. Constatine*, 43 Wash. 102, 86 P. 384 (1906).

*State v. Corporation of Shelbyville*, 36 Tenn. 176 (1856).

*State v. First Nat'l Bank*, 2 S.D. 568, 51 N.W. 587 (1892).

*State v. Lindberg*, 125 Wash. 51, 215 P. 41 (1923).

*State v. Morris Canal & Banking Co.*, 22 N.J.L. 537 (1850).

*State v. Morris & E. R. Co.*, 23 N.J.L. 360 (1852).

*State v. Nicolls*, 61 Wash. 142, 112 P. 269 (1910).

Stewart, James B., "S.E.C. Has a Message for Firms Not Used to Admitting Guilt," *New York Times*, June 21, 2013. As of September 20, 2014: http://www.nytimes.com/2013/06/22/business/secs-new-chief-promises-tougher-line-on-cases.html

Stith, Kate, and José A. Cabranes, *Fear of Judging: Sentencing Guidelines in the Federal Courts*, Chicago, Ill.: University of Chicago Press, 1998.

Suarez, John Peter, assistant administrator of the U.S. Environmental Protection Agency, "Guidance Concerning the Use of Third Parties in the Performance of Supplemental Environmental Projects (SEPs) and the Aggregation of SEP Funds," memorandum to regional counsels for regions I–X, regional enforcement managers for regions I–X, regional media division directors for regions I–X, and regional enforcement coordinators for regions I–X, December 15, 2003. As of September 20, 2014:
http://www2.epa.gov/sites/production/files/documents/seps-thirdparties.pdf

Taibbi, Matt, "Gangster Bankers: Too Big to Jail," *Rolling Stone*, February 14, 2013. As of September 20, 2014:
http://www.rollingstone.com/politics/news/gangster-bankers-too-big-to-jail-20130214

*Tenement House Dep't v. McDevitt*, 215 N.Y. 160, 109 N.E. 88 (1915).

*The Chestnut Hill Turnpike Co. v. Rutter*, 4 Serg. & Rawl. 6 (Pa. 1818).

"The Kindness of Cronies," *New York Times*, editorial, May 25, 2008. As of September 20, 2014:
http://www.nytimes.com/2008/05/25/opinion/25sun3.html

*The King v. Inhabitants of Clifton*, 101 Eng. Rep. 280 (K.B. 1794).

*The Queen v. Birmingham & Gloucester Ry.*, 114 Eng. Rep. 492 (Q.B. 1842).

*The Queen v. Stephens*, L.R. 1 Q.B. 702 (1866).

*The Untouchables*, PBS, January 22, 2013. As of September 20, 2014:
http://www.pbs.org/wgbh/pages/frontline/untouchables/

Thompson, Larry D., deputy attorney general, "Principles of Federal Prosecution of Business Organizations," memorandum to heads of department components and U.S. Attorneys, January 20, 2003.

TRAC—*See* Transactional Records Access Clearinghouse.

Tran, Mark, "Congress to Investigate Mass Enron Paper Shred," *Guardian*, January 21, 2002. As of September 20, 2014:
http://www.theguardian.com/business/2002/jan/21/corporatefraud.enron1

Transactional Records Access Clearinghouse, "TRACFED," undated (a). As of September 20, 2014:
http://tracfed.syr.edu/

———, "About the Data: Judging the Quality of Government Data," undated (b); referenced November 29, 2012. As of September 20, 2014:
http://trac.syr.edu/data/about/judgingQuality.html

———, "The Quick-Start Guide to TRAC and TRACFED," undated (c); referenced November 28, 2012. As of September 20, 2014:
http://trac.syr.edu/guides/quickstart.pdf

———, "Department of Justice Ordered to Release Additional Information," press release, September 13, 2006; referenced November 29, 2012. As of September 20, 2014:
http://trac.syr.edu/foia/eousa/20060913/

*United States v. Agosto-Vega*, 617 F.3d 541 (1st Cir. 2010).

*United States v. Alaska Packers Asso.*, 1 Alaska 217 (1901).

*United States v. Andersen*, 374 F. 3d 281 (5th Cir. 2004).

*United States v. Automated Medical Laboratories, Inc.*, 770 F.2d 399 (4th Cir. 1985).

*United States v. Dotterweich*, 320 U.S. 277, 64 S. Ct. 134 (1943).

*United States v. MacAndrews & Forbes Co.*, 149 F. 823 (S.D.N.Y. 1906).

*United States v. Nearing*, 252 F. 223 (S.D.N.Y. 1918).

*United States v. Park*, 421 U.S. 658 (1975).

*United States v. Potter*, 463 F.3d 9 (1st Cir. 2006).

*United States v. Sain*, 141 F.3d 463 (3rd Cir. 1998).

*United States v. Singh*, 518 F.3d 236 (4th Cir. 2008).

*United States v. Stein*, 495 F. Supp. 2d 390 (S.D.N.Y. 2007).

*United States v. United States Gypsum Co.*, 438 U.S. 422 (1978).

U.S. Attorney's Office for the Eastern District of New York, "Two Former Directors of the New York Racing Association's Pari-Mutuel Department Plead Guilty to Scheme to Defraud the United States," press release, May 6, 2004. As of September 20, 2014:
http://www.usdoj.gov/tax/usaopress/2004/txdv042004may06.htm

U.S. Code, Title 7, Agriculture, Chapter 1, Commodity Exchanges, Section 4, 1976.

———, Title 7, Agriculture, Chapter 19, Cotton Statistics and Estimates, Section 473c-3, Liability of principal for act of agent, 1976.

———, Title 7, Agriculture, Chapter 20, Dumping or Destruction of Interstate Produce, Section 491, Destruction or Dumping of Farm Produce Received in Interstate Commerce by Commission Merchants, etc.; Penalty, 1976.

———, Title 7, Agriculture, Chapter 21, Tobacco Statistics, Section 503, Reports; Necessity; by Whom Made; Penalties, 1976.

———, Title 12, Banks and Banking, Chapter 3, Federal Reserve System, Subchapter X, Powers and Duties of Member Banks, Section 378, Dealers in Securities Engaging in Banking Business; Individuals or Associations Engaging in Banking Business; Examinations and Reports; Penalties, 1976.

———, Title 15, Commerce and Trade, Chapter 1, Monopolies and Combinations in Restraint of Trade, Section 1, Trusts, etc., in Restraint of Trade Illegal; Penalty, 1976.

———, Title 15, Commerce and Trade, Chapter 1, Monopolies and Combinations in Restraint of Trade, Section 2, Monopolizing Trade a Felony; Penalty, 1976.

———, Title 15, Commerce and Trade, Chapter 1, Monopolies and Combinations in Restraint of Trade, Section 3, Trusts in Territories or District of Columbia Illegal; Combination a Felony, 1976.

———, Title 15, Commerce and Trade, Chapter 1, Monopolies and Combinations in Restraint of Trade, Section 7, "Person" or "Persons" Defined, 1976.

———, Title 15, Commerce and Trade, Chapter 2, Federal Trade Commission; Promotion of Export Trade and Prevention of Unfair Methods of Competition, Subchapter I, Federal Trade Commission, Section 50, Offenses and Penalties, 1976.

———, Title 15, Commerce and Trade, Chapter 2, Federal Trade Commission; Promotion of Export Trade and Prevention of Unfair Methods of Competition, Subchapter I, Federal Trade Commission, Section 54, False Advertisements; Penalties, 1976.

———, Title 15, Commerce and Trade, Chapter 2A, Securities and Trust Indentures, Subchapter I, Domestic Securities, Section 77b, Definitions; Promotion of Efficiency, Competition, and Capital Formation, 1976.

———, Title 15, Commerce and Trade, Chapter 2A, Securities and Trust Indentures, Subchapter III, Trust Indentures, Section 77yyy, Penalties, 1976.

———, Title 15, Commerce and Trade, Chapter 2B, Securities Exchanges, Section 78c, Definitions and Application, 1976.

———, Title 15, Commerce and Trade, Chapter 2B, Securities Exchanges, Section 78dd-1, Prohibited Foreign Trade Practices by Issuers, 1976.

———, Title 15, Commerce and Trade, Chapter 2B, Securities Exchanges, Section 78dd-2, Prohibited Foreign Trade Practices by Domestic Concerns, 1976.

———, Title 15, Commerce and Trade, Chapter 2B, Securities Exchanges, Section 78ff, Penalties, 1976.

———, Title 15, Commerce and Trade, Chapter 15, Economic Recovery, Subchapter II, Commodity Credit Corporation, Section 714m, Crimes and Offenses, 1976.

———, Title 15, Commerce and Trade, Chapter 16A, Emergency Petroleum Allocation, Section 754, Omitted, 1976.

———, Title 15, Commerce and Trade, Chapter 53, Toxic Substances Control, Subchapter I, Control of Toxic Substances, Section 2614, Prohibited Acts, 1976.

———, Title 15, Commerce and Trade, Chapter 53, Toxic Substances Control, Subchapter I, Control of Toxic Substances, Section 2615, Penalties, 1976.

———, Title 15, Commerce and Trade, Chapter 98, Public Company Accounting Reform and Corporate Responsibility, Subchapter I, Public Company Accounting Oversight Board, Section 7215, Investigations and Disciplinary Proceedings, 1976.

———, Title 18, Crimes and Criminal Procedure, Part I, Crimes, Chapter 1, General Provisions, Section 2, Principals, 1976.

———, Title 18, Crimes and Criminal Procedure, Part I, Crimes, Chapter 19, Conspiracy, Section 371, Conspiracy to Commit Offense or to Defraud United States, 1976.

———, Title 18, Crimes and Criminal Procedure, Part I, Crimes, Chapter 31, Embezzlement and Theft, Section 657, Lending, Credit and Insurance Institutions, 1976.

———, Title 18, Crimes and Criminal Procedure, Part I, Crimes, Chapter 47, Fraud and False Statements, Section 1014, Loan and Credit Applications Generally; Renewals and Discounts; Crop Insurance, 1976.

———, Title 18, Crimes and Criminal Procedure, Part I, Crimes, Chapter 63, Mail Fraud and Other Fraud Offenses, Section 1348, Securities and Commodities Fraud, 1976.

———, Title 18, Crimes and Criminal Procedure, Part I, Crimes, Chapter 63, Mail Fraud and Other Fraud Offenses, Section 1349, Attempt and Conspiracy, 1976.

———, Title 18, Crimes and Criminal Procedure, Part I, Crimes, Chapter 63, Mail Fraud and Other Fraud Offenses, Section 1350, Failure of Corporate Officers to Certify Financial Reports, 1976.

———, Title 18, Crimes and Criminal Procedure, Part I, Crimes, Chapter 73, Obstruction of Justice, Section 1512, Tampering with a Witness, Victim, or an Informant, 1976.

———, Title 18, Crimes and Criminal Procedure, Part I, Crimes, Chapter 73, Obstruction of Justice, Section 1514A, Civil Action to Protect Against Retaliation in Fraud Cases, 1976.

———, Title 18, Crimes and Criminal Procedure, Part I, Crimes, Chapter 73, Obstruction of Justice, Section 1519, Destruction, Alteration, or Falsification of Records in Federal Investigations and Bankruptcy, 1976.

———, Title 18, Crimes and Criminal Procedure, Part I, Crimes, Chapter 73, Obstruction of Justice, Section 1520, Destruction of Corporate Audit Records, 1976.

———, Title 18, Crimes and Criminal Procedure, Part I, Crimes, Chapter 90, Protection of Trade Secrets, Section 1832, Theft of Trade Secrets, 1976.

———, Title 21, Food and Drugs, Chapter 4, Animals, Meats, and Meat and Dairy Products, Subchapter I, Examination of Animals, Meats, and Meat and Dairy Products, Section 88, 1976.

———, Title 21, Food and Drugs, Chapter 4, Animals, Meats, and Meat and Dairy Products, Subchapter I, Examination of Animals, Meats, and Meat and Dairy Products, Section 90, 1976.

———, Title 21, Food and Drugs, Chapter 9, Federal Food, Drug, and Cosmetic Act, Subchapter II, Definitions, Section 321, Definitions; Generally, 1976.

———, Title 21, Food and Drugs, Chapter 12, Meat Inspection, Subchapter I, Inspection Requirements; Adulteration and Misbranding, Section 602, Congressional Statement of Findings, 1976.

———, Title 21, Food and Drugs, Chapter 12, Meat Inspection, Subchapter I, Inspection Requirements; Adulteration and Misbranding, Section 610, Prohibited Acts, 1976.

———, Title 21, Food and Drugs, Chapter 12, Meat Inspection, Subchapter I, Inspection Requirements; Adulteration and Misbranding, Section 611, Devices, Marks, Labels, and Certificates; Simulations, 1976.

———, Title 21, Food and Drugs, Chapter 12, Meat Inspection, Subchapter IV, Auxiliary Provisions, Section 676, Violations, 1976.

———, Title 28, Judiciary and Judicial Procedure, Part III, Court Officers and Employees, Chapter 58, United States Sentencing Commission, Section 991, United States Sentencing Commission; Establishment and Purposes, 1988.

———, Title 29, Labor, Chapter 8, Fair Labor Standards, Section 215, Prohibited Acts; Prima Facie Evidence, 1976.

———, Title 29, Labor, Chapter 11, Labor-Management Reporting and Disclosure Procedure, Subchapter III, Reporting by Labor Organizations, Officers and Employees of Labor Organizations, and Employers, Section 433, Report of Employers, 1976.

———, Title 33, Navigation and Navigable Waters, Chapter 1, Navigable Waters Generally, Subchapter I, General Provisions, Section 1, Regulations by Secretary of the Army for Navigation of Waters Generally, 1976.

———, Title 33, Navigation and Navigable Waters, Chapter 1, Navigable Waters Generally, Subchapter I, General Provisions, Section 3, Regulations to Prevent Injuries from Target Practice, 1976.

———, Title 33, Navigation and Navigable Waters, Chapter 9, Protection of Navigable Waters and of Harbor and River Improvements Generally, Subchapter I, In General, Section 406, Penalty for Wrongful Construction of Bridges, Piers, etc.; Removal of Structures, 1976.

———, Title 33, Navigation and Navigable Waters, Chapter 9, Protection of Navigable Waters and of Harbor and River Improvements Generally, Subchapter I, In General, Section 411, Penalty for Wrongful Deposit of Refuse; Use of or Injury to Harbor Improvements, and Obstruction of Navigable Waters Generally, 1976.

———, Title 33, Navigation and Navigable Waters, Chapter 9, Protection of Navigable Waters and of Harbor and River Improvements Generally, Subchapter I, In General, Section 419, Regulation by Secretary Governing Transportation and Dumping of Dredgings, Refuse, etc., into Navigable Waters; Oyster Lands; Appropriations, 1976.

———, Title 33, Navigation and Navigable Waters, Chapter 9, Protection of Navigable Waters and of Harbor and River Improvements Generally, Subchapter III, New York Harbor, Harbor of Hampton Roads, and Harbor of Baltimore, Section 449, Disposition of Dredged Matter; Persons Liable; Penalty, 1976.

———, Title 33, Navigation and Navigable Waters, Chapter 12, River and Harbor Improvements Generally, Subchapter IV, Particular Work or Improvements, Section 602, Maintenance of Channel of South Pass of Mississippi River, 1976.

———, Title 33, Navigation and Navigable Waters, Chapter 20, Pollution of the Sea by Oil, Section 1001, 1976.

———, Title 33, Navigation and Navigable Waters, Chapter 20, Pollution of the Sea by Oil, Section 1005, 1976.

———, Title 33, Navigation and Navigable Waters, Chapter 26, Water Pollution Prevention and Control, Subchapter III, Standards and Enforcement, Section 1319, Enforcement, 1976.

———, Title 41, Public Contracts, Chapter 1, General Provisions, Section 52, Definitions, 1976.

———, Title 47, Telecommunications, Chapter 5, Wire or Radio Communication, Subchapter II, Common Carriers, Part I, Common Carrier Regulation, Section 217, Agents' Acts and Omissions; Liability of Carrier, 1976.

U.S. Department of Justice, Office of Justice Programs, Bureau of Justice Statistics, *Federal Justice Statistics Program: Defendants in Federal Criminal Cases: Terminated, 1994*, Ann Arbor, Mich.: Inter-university Consortium for Political and Social Research, March 8, 2011a. As of October 27, 2014: http://www.icpsr.umich.edu/icpsrweb/NACJD/studies/23743

———, *Federal Justice Statistics Program: Defendants in Federal Criminal Cases: Terminated, 1995*, Ann Arbor, Mich.: Inter-university Consortium for Political and Social Research, March 8, 2011b. As of October 27, 2014:
http://www.icpsr.umich.edu/icpsrweb/NACJD/studies/24008

———, *Federal Justice Statistics Program: Defendants in Federal Criminal Cases: Terminated, 1996*, Ann Arbor, Mich.: Inter-university Consortium for Political and Social Research, March 8, 2011c. As of October 27, 2014:
http://www.icpsr.umich.edu/icpsrweb/NACJD/studies/24027

———, *Federal Justice Statistics Program: Defendants in Federal Criminal Cases: Terminated, 1997*, Ann Arbor, Mich.: Inter-university Consortium for Political and Social Research, March 8, 2011d. As of October 27, 2014:
http://www.icpsr.umich.edu/icpsrweb/NACJD/studies/24046

———, *Federal Justice Statistics Program: Defendants in Federal Criminal Cases: Terminated, 1998*, Ann Arbor, Mich.: Inter-university Consortium for Political and Social Research, March 8, 2011e. As of October 27, 2014:
http://www.icpsr.umich.edu/icpsrweb/NACJD/studies/24065

———, *Federal Justice Statistics Program: Defendants in Federal Criminal Cases: Terminated, 1999*, Ann Arbor, Mich.: Inter-university Consortium for Political and Social Research, March 8, 2011f. As of October 27, 2014:
http://www.icpsr.umich.edu/icpsrweb/NACJD/studies/24084

———, *Federal Justice Statistics Program: Defendants in Federal Criminal Cases: Terminated, 2000*, Ann Arbor, Mich.: Inter-university Consortium for Political and Social Research, March 8, 2011g. As of October 27, 2014:
http://www.icpsr.umich.edu/icpsrweb/NACJD/studies/24103

———, *Federal Justice Statistics Program: Defendants in Federal Criminal Cases: Terminated, 2001*, Ann Arbor, Mich.: Inter-university Consortium for Political and Social Research, March 8, 2011h. As of October 27, 2014:
http://www.icpsr.umich.edu/icpsrweb/NACJD/studies/24122

———, *Federal Justice Statistics Program: Defendants in Federal Criminal Cases: Terminated, 2002*, Ann Arbor, Mich.: Inter-university Consortium for Political and Social Research, March 8, 2011i. As of October 27, 2014:
http://www.icpsr.umich.edu/icpsrweb/NACJD/studies/24141

———, *Federal Justice Statistics Program: Defendants in Federal Criminal Cases: Terminated, 2003*, Ann Arbor, Mich.: Inter-university Consortium for Political and Social Research, March 8, 2011j. As of October 27, 2014:
http://www.icpsr.umich.edu/icpsrweb/NACJD/studies/24160

———, *Federal Justice Statistics Program: Defendants in Federal Criminal Cases: Terminated, 2004*, Ann Arbor, Mich.: Inter-university Consortium for Political and Social Research, March 8, 2011k. As of October 27, 2014:
http://www.icpsr.umich.edu/icpsrweb/NACJD/studies/24177

———, *Federal Justice Statistics Program: Defendants in Federal Criminal Cases: Terminated, 2005*, Ann Arbor, Mich.: Inter-university Consortium for Political and Social Research, March 8, 2011l. As of October 27, 2014: http://www.icpsr.umich.edu/icpsrweb/NACJD/studies/24195

———, *Federal Justice Statistics Program: Defendants in Federal Criminal Cases: Terminated, 2006*, Ann Arbor, Mich.: Inter-university Consortium for Political and Social Research, March 8, 2011m. As of October 27, 2014: http://www.icpsr.umich.edu/icpsrweb/NACJD/studies/24212

———, *Federal Justice Statistics Program: Defendants in Federal Criminal Cases: Terminated, 2007*, Ann Arbor, Mich.: Inter-university Consortium for Political and Social Research, March 8, 2011n. As of October 27, 2014: http://www.icpsr.umich.edu/icpsrweb/NACJD/studies/24227

———, *Federal Justice Statistics Program: Defendants in Federal Criminal Cases: Terminated, 2008*, Ann Arbor, Mich.: Inter-university Consortium for Political and Social Research, March 8, 2011o. As of October 27, 2014: http://www.icpsr.umich.edu/icpsrweb/NACJD/studies/29433

———, *Federal Justice Statistics Program: Suspects in Federal Criminal Matters Concluded, 1994*, Ann Arbor, Mich.: Inter-university Consortium for Political and Social Research, March 8, 2011p. As of October 27, 2014: http://www.icpsr.umich.edu/icpsrweb/NACJD/studies/23741

———, *Federal Justice Statistics Program: Suspects in Federal Criminal Matters Concluded, 1995*, Ann Arbor, Mich.: Inter-university Consortium for Political and Social Research, March 8, 2011q. As of October 27, 2014: http://www.icpsr.umich.edu/icpsrweb/NACJD/studies/24006

———, *Federal Justice Statistics Program: Suspects in Federal Criminal Matters Concluded, 1996*, Ann Arbor, Mich.: Inter-university Consortium for Political and Social Research, March 8, 2011r. As of October 27, 2014: http://www.icpsr.umich.edu/icpsrweb/NACJD/studies/24025

———, *Federal Justice Statistics Program: Suspects in Federal Criminal Matters Concluded, 1997*, Ann Arbor, Mich.: Inter-university Consortium for Political and Social Research, March 8, 2011s. As of October 27, 2014: http://www.icpsr.umich.edu/icpsrweb/NACJD/studies/24044

———, *Federal Justice Statistics Program: Suspects in Federal Criminal Matters Concluded, 1998*, Ann Arbor, Mich.: Inter-university Consortium for Political and Social Research, March 8, 2011t. As of October 27, 2014: http://www.icpsr.umich.edu/icpsrweb/NACJD/studies/24063

———, *Federal Justice Statistics Program: Suspects in Federal Criminal Matters Concluded, 1999*, Ann Arbor, Mich.: Inter-university Consortium for Political and Social Research, March 8, 2011u. As of October 27, 2014: http://www.icpsr.umich.edu/icpsrweb/NACJD/studies/24082

———, *Federal Justice Statistics Program: Suspects in Federal Criminal Matters Concluded, 2000*, Ann Arbor, Mich.: Inter-university Consortium for Political and Social Research, March 8, 2011v. As of October 27, 2014: http://www.icpsr.umich.edu/icpsrweb/NACJD/studies/24101

———, *Federal Justice Statistics Program: Suspects in Federal Criminal Matters Concluded, 2001*, Ann Arbor, Mich.: Inter-university Consortium for Political and Social Research, March 8, 2011w. As of October 27, 2014: http://www.icpsr.umich.edu/icpsrweb/NACJD/studies/24120

———, *Federal Justice Statistics Program: Suspects in Federal Criminal Matters Concluded, 2002*, Ann Arbor, Mich.: Inter-university Consortium for Political and Social Research, March 8, 2011x. As of October 27, 2014: http://www.icpsr.umich.edu/icpsrweb/NACJD/studies/24139

———, *Federal Justice Statistics Program: Suspects in Federal Criminal Matters Concluded, 2003*, Ann Arbor, Mich.: Inter-university Consortium for Political and Social Research, March 8, 2011y. As of October 27, 2014: http://www.icpsr.umich.edu/icpsrweb/NACJD/studies/24158

———, *Federal Justice Statistics Program: Suspects in Federal Criminal Matters Concluded, 2004*, Ann Arbor, Mich.: Inter-university Consortium for Political and Social Research, March 8, 2011z. As of October 27, 2014: http://www.icpsr.umich.edu/icpsrweb/NACJD/studies/24175

———, *Federal Justice Statistics Program: Suspects in Federal Criminal Matters Concluded, 2005*, Ann Arbor, Mich.: Inter-university Consortium for Political and Social Research, March 8, 2011aa. As of October 27, 2014: http://www.icpsr.umich.edu/icpsrweb/NACJD/studies/24193

———, *Federal Justice Statistics Program: Suspects in Federal Criminal Matters Concluded, 2006*, Ann Arbor, Mich.: Inter-university Consortium for Political and Social Research, March 8, 2011bb. As of October 27, 2014: http://www.icpsr.umich.edu/icpsrweb/NACJD/studies/24210

———, *Federal Justice Statistics Program: Suspects in Federal Criminal Matters Concluded, 2007*, Ann Arbor, Mich.: Inter-university Consortium for Political and Social Research, March 8, 2011cc. As of October 27, 2014: http://www.icpsr.umich.edu/icpsrweb/NACJD/studies/24225

———, *Federal Justice Statistics Program: Suspects in Federal Criminal Matters Concluded, 2008*, Ann Arbor, Mich.: Inter-university Consortium for Political and Social Research, March 8, 2011dd. As of October 27, 2014: http://www.icpsr.umich.edu/icpsrweb/NACJD/studies/29424

———, *Federal Justice Statistics Program: Defendants Charged in Criminal Cases Filed in District Court, 2009*, Ann Arbor, Mich.: Inter-university Consortium for Political and Social Research, June 3, 2011ee. As of September 20, 2014: http://www.icpsr.umich.edu/icpsrweb/NACJD/studies/30791/detail

———, *Federal Justice Statistics Program: Defendants in Federal Criminal Cases Filed in District Court, 2009*, Ann Arbor, Mich.: Inter-university Consortium for Political and Social Research, June 3, 2011ff. As of September 20, 2014:
http://www.icpsr.umich.edu/icpsrweb/NACJD/studies/30781/detail

———, *Federal Justice Statistics Program: Defendants in Federal Criminal Cases: Terminated, 2009*, Ann Arbor, Mich.: Inter-university Consortium for Political and Social Research, June 3, 2011gg. As of October 27, 2014:
http://www.icpsr.umich.edu/icpsrweb/NACJD/studies/29433

———, *Federal Justice Statistics Program: Suspects in Federal Criminal Matters Concluded, 2009*, Ann Arbor, Mich.: Inter-university Consortium for Political and Social Research, June 3, 2011hh. As of October 27, 2014:
http://www.icpsr.umich.edu/icpsrweb/NACJD/studies/30790

U.S. Senate, *P.L. 98-473, Continuing Appropriations, 1985—Comprehensive Crime Control Act of 1984*, S. Rep. 98-225, August 4, 1983.

U.S. Sentencing Commission, *Supplementary Report on the Initial Sentencing Guidelines and Policy Statements*, June 18, 1987.

———, "Sentencing Guidelines for United States Courts," *Federal Register*, Vol. 63, No. 229, November 30, 1998, pp. 65979–65993. As of September 20, 2014:
http://www.gpo.gov/fdsys/pkg/FR-1998-11-30/html/98-31756.htm

———, *Organizations Convicted in Federal Criminal Courts, 1999–2008*, Washington, D.C., 1999.

———, "Sentencing Guidelines for United States Courts," *Federal Register*, Vol. 66, No. 109, June 6, 2001, pp. 30512–30563. As of September 20, 2014:
http://www.gpo.gov/fdsys/granule/FR-2001-06-06/01-13966

———, *2009 Annual Report*, c. 2009. As of September 20, 2014:
http://www.ussc.gov/research-and-publications/annual-reports-sourcebooks/2009/annual-report-2009

———, *Federal Sentencing Guidelines Manual*, Washington, D.C., 2011. As of September 29, 2014:
http://www.ussc.gov/guidelines-manual/2011-federal-sentencing-guidelines-manual

———, *2012 USSC Guidelines Manual*, 2012. As of September 20, 2014:
http://www.ussc.gov/guidelines-manual/2012-ussc-guidelines-manual

———, "Sentencing of Organizations," *Guidelines Manual*, 2013. As of October 27, 2014:
http://www.ussc.gov/guidelines-manual/2013-ussc-guidelines-manual

Viswantatha, Aruna, and Nate Raymond, "Holder Asks Congress for Help in Fighting Wall Street Crime," *Pittsburgh Post-Gazette*, September 18, 2014, p. A6.

White, Mary Jo, "Corporate Criminal Liability: What Has Gone Wrong?" *37th Annual Institute on Securities Regulation*, Vol. 2, November 2005, pp. 815–828.

Williams, Glanville Llewellyn, *Criminal Law: The General Part*, 2nd ed., London: Stevens, 1961.